Outside of the 9 to 5

Your practical guide to designing
and building a profitable business
that gives you freedom,
flexibility, and fulfilment

ANNA S. E. LUNDBERG

To all those who dream of a life outside of the '9 to 5'.

CONTENTS

PREFACE

In October 2018, I fulfilled a lifelong ambition to publish my own book. *Leaving the Corporate 9 to 5* was a collection of stories of people who had quit their jobs to forge their own path. Having quit my own corporate marketing job in 2013, I was fascinated by these stories, in which everyone shared how they had come to make the decision to quit, the key challenges they had faced and how they had overcome those challenges, and any advice they'd give to someone who was considering doing the same.

The book was intended to inspire people with the possibilities that were out there and reassure them that they were not alone in looking for an alternative. I always felt, however, that there was something missing. While it was full of useful tips and titbits, I wanted to provide a more practical guide as how to you might go about building that life outside of the 9 to 5. As my own business evolved, I also became more aware of the ongoing challenges of sustaining a life and business outside of the 9 to 5.

With almost a decade of experience now facing these challenges myself as well as supporting clients, my thinking has evolved, and my guidance has become more structured and comprehensive. This book represents a consolidation of that experience and expertise, as I take you through how to design and build a profitable business that brings you more freedom, flexibility, and fulfilment – outside of the 9 to 5.

ACKNOWLEDGEMENTS

Thank you to all my clients, who have trusted me to guide them on building their own version of a life outside of the 9 to 5, and who have implemented and validated my strategies and frameworks. Thanks also to those in my community who have supported, and are continuing to support, me on my own personal and professional journey.

Introduction

INTRODUCTION

In 2013, I quit my corporate marketing job. I had ended up there 'accidentally', having studied PPE (Philosophy, Politics, and Economics) at the University of Oxford followed by International Relations at the Graduate Institute of International Studies in Geneva, Switzerland.

There were what I now call 'push' reasons driving me out of the corporate 9 to 5. A competitive culture that, although it suited me as a high achiever, didn't always feel so healthy. A product that I didn't see as making a positive contribution in the world. And a career path where I didn't see myself on the higher rungs of the ladder, in the roles of the more senior directors and general managers of the organisation.

There were also what I call 'pull' reasons drawing me towards something else. More freedom in how I worked and, more generally, how I lived my life. More flexibility in when and where I worked. And more fulfilment in terms of the kind of work that I was doing.

As a first step, I had the idea to ask my boss for a sabbatical, and off I went to travel by myself for three months across South America. I sailed the Galapagos islands, hiked the Inca Trail to Machu Picchu, and drove across the salt plains of Bolivia. Along the way, I immersed myself in all things career and life choices. I met people from different walks of life, with different backgrounds and different aspirations. And, halfway through that trip, I called up my line manager and officially handed in my resignation.

Having only had a vague idea of what exactly I wanted to do instead, I was lucky to land on my feet as a digital marketing consultant. I was able to use my skills, experience, and network to earn a generous income working with other companies and guiding them on strategy, training, and implementation. I soon realised, however, that although this was a step in the right direction, it wasn't giving me that freedom, flexibility, and fulfilment that I was longing for.

OUTSIDE OF THE 9 TO 5

I 'quit' my own consulting business and off I went on more adventures. I trained and certified as a coach and launched my coaching and mentoring business in 2015. I wrote articles and, over time, learned how to do things like email marketing, Facebook groups, and Instagram graphics. I published my book, *Leaving the Corporate 9 to 5*, in October 2018 and launched my podcast Reimagining Success™ a couple of months later.

Things also evolved on a personal level. Having been single and 'carefree' when I initially quit my job and started to travel, over the next couple of years, I fell in love and settled down in London. My partner and I had a daughter, and then a son, and in 2021 we moved down to the south coast. As I finish writing this book, I've just turned the big 4-0. My vision for what I want my life to look like, and how I will go about creating that, has shifted and continues to evolve.

Outside of the 9 to 5

As it turns out, deciding that you want to create a career and life for yourself outside of the 9 to 5 – deciding to quit your job and start a business – is only the beginning. It's a massive step, and requires a lot of courage and commitment, but it is just the very first step.

Following that decision, you may find that you experience overwhelm when faced with all the different possibilities for what to do next; doubts as to whether you're doing the right thing, especially through the inevitable dips in confidence and results; frustration when you're working with difficult clients and not getting paid enough; anxiety as you wonder where your next client will come from, and when; and, if you push yourself too much, stress to the point of burnout.

Through the twists and turns of my own transition out of my corporate employment and into working for myself, and through supporting my clients and community over the past decade, I've identified five key areas that you need to focus on to make your escape plan, and your business, viable for the long term. If you're lacking in one or more of these areas, then

you're probably struggling with some aspect of the escape process.

This is not just about financial success but about creating something that is meaningful, enjoyable, and manageable in the context of all the other things (and people) that are important in your life.

The 5 Pillars

The 5 Pillars represent these 5 areas that you need to focus on to build a business, and a life, outside of the 9 to 5. They are a consolidation of everything that I've learned through my own experience and the experiences of my clients.

The 5 Pillars are:

PILLAR 1: Identifying your personal definition of success – are you crystal clear on what really matters in your life and business?

PILLAR 2: Cultivating confidence and resilience – do you feel equipped to deal with the inevitable ups and downs?

PILLAR 3: Choosing the right business model – do you have a plan for the successful operation of your business?

PILLAR 4: Building an effective personal brand – are you building an effective platform to consistently attract clients?

PILLAR 5: Designing flexible work-life integration – have you found a way to balance your business with everything else?

I'm convinced that these 5 Pillars contain all the ingredients that you'll need to make your business work, and make it work for you.

How to use the book

The book is structured around the 5 Pillars: your definition of success; confidence and resilience; business model; personal brand; and work-life integration. You might be tempted, and you are very welcome, to jump to the section that most interests you, or where you feel that you need the most work.

The 5 Pillars are not directly sequential as such and, in fact, you will need to eventually work on them in parallel.

I do recommend, however, that you start with the first foundational pillar, where you will identify – or refine – your personal definition of success. Without this clear vision for what you want your business and your life to look like, any other work that you do may take you off in the wrong direction. Get clear on where you want to go, and then you can work out how you're going to get there.

If you're just starting out and you want to get the foundations right from day one, this book will help you get that solid base on which to build a business that will last. If you've been in business for a while but you're not quite achieving the freedom, flexibility, and fulfilment that you're after, this book will help you revisit some of those foundations and ask the right questions to ensure that you're building the business that you dreamed of when you started.

Each of the 5 Pillars consists of four steps; and each of those steps has a set of exercises at the end of the chapter. These exercises will help you apply what you've been reading to your own life and business.

If you do want to take things further, I've included some resources at the back of the book. I'd like to draw your attention to two of these in particular.

First, you can get a free assessment of your business. The 5 Pillars scorecard includes a simple checklist with statements that will help you evaluate where the gaps are, along with clear indicated actions to help you close those gaps and build the business and life that you're after. Download the scorecard at onestepoutside.com/scorecard.

Second, if you'd like to work through the materials on the 5 Pillars in a structured course along with an interactive workbook to support your learning, please consider the Outsiders Business Academy. This is a self-paced course for you to work through in your own time, to learn – and implement – the foundations of building a profitable business that lets you escape the 9 to 5. Register and start learning now at onestepoutside.com/course.

Here's to your success – whatever 'success' means to you.

Anna Lundberg, Poole 14th December 2022

What is a life 'outside of the 9 to 5'?

WHAT IS A LIFE 'OUTSIDE OF THE 9 TO 5'?

This book will guide you on how to design and build a business, and a life, outside of the 9 to 5. But why would you want to build such a life, and what does it look like?

I imagine, given that you've picked up this book and you're now reading it, that you have a bit of an idea. But I'd like to dig into what I mean by this life 'outside of the 9 to 5', to give the context for how I recommend you go about making it happen.

Of course, before we can define a life 'outside of the 9 to 5', we must first define what 'inside the 9 to 5' looks like. In my previous book, *Leaving the Corporate 9 to 5*, I defined the 'corporate 9 to 5' as encompassing the following parameters:

- working in a private corporation, the primary motivation of which is profit and in which you are a small part of a big machine;
- working in an office-type environment;
- reporting to a more senior manager (your boss);
- working standard hours of Monday to Friday, traditionally 9am to 5pm but now usually involving longer days and, thanks to technology, work from home in the evenings and on the weekends; and
- receiving a regular monthly salary and other benefits such as insurance and a pension.

I suggested that alternatives to this 'corporate 9 to 5' could include:

- working in a different type of company or organisation, with different motivations;
- working at home or in a different environment;
- working for yourself or for a number of different clients;
- working atypical hours (something that is increasingly possible now within some companies, with the growth of flexible and hybrid working arrangements); and
- no longer receiving a regular salary and benefits.

In that first book, I presented five possible alternatives and shared stories of people who had (i) moved into a different sector; (ii) gone freelance; (iii) launched their own business; (iv) created a portfolio career; or (v) taken a leap of faith, not knowing exactly what it would lead to.

The '9 to 5' is not just a function of the hours that you're working, or even the office environment where you spend your days. It represents something bigger, a whole set of expectations for how you should be working and, by extension, how you should be living your life. It involves accepting the 'Sunday scaries' and 'Monday blues' as an unavoidable part of your weekly routine, as you count the days until the weekend ("TGIF!") and the weeks until your next holiday. It sets an expectation that you must be always busy, always 'on', and never able to disconnect, with endless meetings and an overflowing email inbox. And it measures productivity by the number of hours that you're working, seeing stress and burnout almost as a badge of honour that proves how important you are.

The pandemic has prompted, or at least accelerated, an awakening where people are questioning whether the 9 to 5 is the right framework for a modern-day service economy. We are looking to spend more quality time with loved ones and demanding more flexibility to be able to do so. And, when we are working, we want to be doing work that really makes a difference.

This is where it gets exciting; and this what I mean by a 'life outside of the 9 to 5'. A life where you are clear on what's important to you and you are dedicating your time and energy to those priorities. Where you have the confidence to go after your biggest dreams and fulfil your true potential. And where you can pursue your ambitions and make a real impact without having to compromise on your health and relationships to do so.

This is what I mean by a life and business outside of the 9 to 5, and it's on that basis that I've developed these 5 Pillars.

So, without further ado, let's get started with Pillar 1: Identifying your personal definition of success.

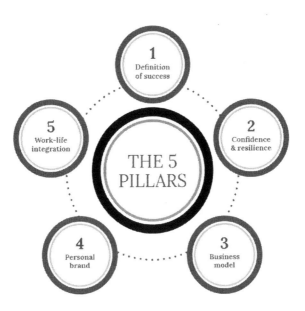

Pillar 1:
Identifying your personal definition of success

PILLAR 1:
IDENTIFYING YOUR PERSONAL DEFINITION OF SUCCESS

Of the 5 Pillars, Pillar 1 is the most important. This first pillar is laying the foundation for everything else in the book, in your business, and in your life. Its underlying message of redefining success is core to what drives me, both personally and professionally, and I'm excited to dive into this with you now.

Did you ever stop to ask yourself, "What does success mean to me?" For most people, the answer is no. Most likely, you'll have been following someone else's definition of success that you've inherited from your parents and family, your teachers and education, or society. That definition has guided your decisions and choices in your life so far, whether consciously or, more likely, subconsciously.

If you haven't been following someone else's definition of success, then you may not have been following any definition of success at all. Without any clear vision of what you're working towards, how are you going to have any hope of ending up somewhere that you want to be?

When it comes to designing a business that allows you to live the life and lifestyle that you want, the danger if you don't define success is that you'll develop an 'accidental' business model. You'll replicate the structures and principles that you're familiar with from your corporate work; perhaps you'll try to copy someone else's apparently successful model; or you'll end up trying all kinds of things with no vision or strategy at all for what you're trying to create.

The result will be a business that will either fail altogether, compelling you to go back to a corporate employer with your tail between your legs, or else a business that is 'successful' but not in a way that is meaningful to you. You will have recreated the same restrictive environment that you experienced in corporate or perhaps, in following someone else's blueprint, you will have ended up with a version of success that doesn't fit with who you are and what you want.

The very first thing for you to think about is what you want and why it's so important to you. So, the first step in Pillar 1 is to get clear on your big picture vision. 'Big picture' means that you're looking not just at what you want from your work, from your business, but from all areas of your life. Work is a part of life – it's an important part, but nonetheless it is just one part of many. We'll start by looking at your vision for how you want to live your life.

Next, we're going to be clarifying your core values. This was one of the very first exercises that my peer coach gave me during my coach training, and one of the most enlightening. I return to it again and again for myself and for my clients. Clarifying your values is going to give you a compass to guide your decisions along the way.

We'll then move onto your purpose. 'Purpose' is a big word, and one that can be quite intimidating. I'll break this down for you and show you how I use it in a very specific and tangible way to help you design your business.

Finally, we'll look at how you can achieve balance. We'll be exploring the idea of 'work-life balance' – or, rather, 'work-life integration', the term that I prefer – in Pillar 5, but I already want to introduce this concept now. I'll be encouraging you to make sure that you have balanced goals across the different areas of your life, rather than focusing single-mindedly on your business.

So, let's get started with identifying your personal definition of success. First up is getting clear on that big picture vision.

GETTING CLEAR ON YOUR 'BIG PICTURE' VISION

Your 'big picture vision' is big, by definition, and it's exciting; this is where you get to imagine your very best life. But, as with everything that's exciting, it's also quite scary, as you allow yourself to question everything you've so far taken for granted and open yourself up to dreaming of something different. It's an important foundation because how on earth can you work out how you're going to get to where you want to be, if you don't know where that is and what that looks like?

So, first of all, let's start with examining this word, 'success'. And a quick Google will give you the following definition:

the attainment of fame, wealth or social status

I imagine that this definition is consistent with your initial perception of 'success'. Most of us would spontaneously associate success with the corporate career ladder and the promotions and salary increases that come with climbing up and up; a big house and a fancy car; and being respected and admired by society, and by your peers.

However, if you go back to that definition on Google, you'll also see the following:

the accomplishment of an aim or purpose

And this is where it gets interesting. This definition means that you get to decide – in fact, you must decide – what your 'aim or purpose' is. Most likely, that's something you haven't been doing, at least not explicitly, so far in your life and career. What is the aim or purpose that you're working towards? And why is it meaningful to you?

Now we begin to question the more superficial definition of success as fame and fortune, and any other definition that you've implicitly inherited from your family and through your formal education. This can be unsettling, but also incredibly empowering, because it means you get to choose your own path. And, by the way, this is something that you'll continue to do in the coming years, as it can and will evolve over time. Right now, we're just going to get started on this journey, one that will continue for the rest of your life.

Escaping the 9 to 5

To make all this big picture thinking a little more concrete, let's zoom in on the specific context of escaping the 9 to 5. What is your 'aim or purpose' here? Why do you want to, or did you already, quit your job? Why do you aspire to this life outside of the 9 to 5? In my experience, there are two sets of drivers, two sets of reasons, why people want to escape the 9 to 5.

The first set of reasons are *push* reasons, meaning the things that are pushing you out of the 9 to 5. These reasons might include a toxic work culture; a 'bad' boss or poor senior management; or a misalignment of values. In more practical terms, there might be a long commute; long working hours where you're having to work late into the evening and into your weekends (9 to 5? More like 7 to 11); and the inevitable consequence of stress and burnout.

These 'push' reasons are pushing you out of the 9 to 5. You're beginning to recognise, that "I don't want to do this anymore," but perhaps you don't yet know what it is you want to do instead. That's okay because that's what we're here to find out. Having an awareness and understanding of your push reasons, what you don't want, is an important first step.

Figure 1: Why do you want to escape the 9 to 5?

The second set of reasons are the *pull* reasons, meaning that you're not just being pushed away from something but you're being drawn, pulled, towards something else.

This is where I talk about "freedom, flexibility, and fulfilment". Greater freedom and autonomy in the work that you do and how you live your life; more flexibility when it comes to when and where you're working; and more meaning and impact from the type of work that you're doing.

So, there are push reasons pushing you out of the 9 to 5 and pull reasons pulling you towards something else. This is the first piece of understanding your 'aim or purpose' when it comes to designing your business.

The meaning of life

One of the many books that I read when I was first starting my own journey out of the 9 to 5 was Victor Frankl's *Man's Search for Meaning* (2004). Frankl was a psychiatrist who survived the Holocaust and its unspeakable horrors, finding his meaning in the work that he did to understand how someone can survive such a horrific experience. One of the biggest insights for me (p. 109) was this:

> *Ultimately, man should not ask what the meaning of his life is, but rather he must recognise that it is* he *who is asked.*

So, yes, we are talking about The Meaning of Life, capital M, capital L, but, more specifically, we are talking about your personal meaning. What is the meaning of *your* life? What is *your* definition of success? What is *your* aim or purpose? And there are a few questions that you can ask yourself here, to get closer to an answer.

Do – Be – Have

What do you want to do, be, and have? The tendency is to focus on the *have* – "I want to have a big house," or "I want to have a successful career" – and this can leave you with quite superficial goals. In focusing only on the things that you want to have in your life, you don't really get to the heart of what you want and why. Here, we're trying to go a bit deeper.

The second part, then, is what do you want to *do*? Maybe you've always wanted to write a book, you want to travel the world, or you want to spend more time with your children?

Finally, what do you want to *be*? Do you want to be seen as a thought leader in your industry, an inspirational role model, or a nurturing parent?

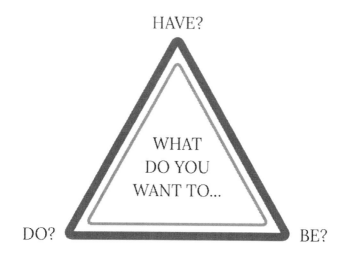

Figure 2: Do – Be – Have

So those are three different elements to look at, to reframe your goals and to try to get closer to your vision by coming at this from a few different angles.

Your ideal day

The next one, and this is a powerful exercise, is asking yourself: What does your ideal day look like?

You wake up in the morning... Maybe there's no alarm, a nice change after years of being tied to a strict schedule at school, university, and work. So, you wake up naturally, with the sunlight streaming in through the big open windows, and you go for a run along the beach. You come back and have a nice cup of coffee and a smoothie – with your partner? With your children? Alone? You have a shower and meditate before sitting down at your desk for a first writing session, because you're working on your next article or book. You meet some friends for lunch at your favourite café. Then, in the afternoon, you're running a workshop, or you're taking client calls. You finish at three and you pick up the kids from school. You go to the park; you come home and have dinner together as a family. Bedtime with a book. Then it's quality time with your partner, a bath, and your latest novel in bed.

What does that ideal day look like for you? Where are you? Who are you with? What are you doing? What is the environment? What does it smell like? Try to visualise your experience in as much sensory detail as you can.

This exercise can give you a lot of insight into what you are missing from your life and routine today. Often, it will also illustrate how easy it would be for you to make small tweaks to your current day to bring it more in line with your ideal.

What if it all works out?

One of the things that can get in the way of all this dreaming and imagining is the doubt and fear that tends to creep in. "That will never work," "I could never…" or "It's too unrealistic." We'll look at this properly in Pillar 2, where we'll work on building your confidence and resilience and specifically break down what we call your "limiting beliefs".

For now, though, let's ask the question, "What if?" What if it all works out exactly as you hope? Forget all the reasons why it might not work and focus instead on the question, what if it does? What would that look like? What could that look like?

Are you living in a tropical paradise with a thriving business, working three days a week? Are you a best-selling author with ten books to your name? What does this best-case scenario look like for you? Once you've allowed yourself to dream with no filter, to get clear on what you really want, then you can start to consider what is and isn't feasible.

Creating your vision board

We'll end this first chapter on your vision with a final exercise that can help you bring it to life in a very visual way: creating a vision board. A vision board is a collection of pictures and text that depicts the elements that we've been talking about here – the do-be-have, the ideal day, the "what if it all works out?" – in a way that's relevant and inspiring to you.

I've created a vision board a few times over the years and, as you can imagine, it looked very different as I first quit my corporate job back in 2013, single and fully focused on my own needs and desires, compared to how it looks today with an existing business to maintain and, most importantly, a partner and two little ones.

How can you represent your vision in a way that is broad and flexible enough so that you can explore different opportunities at this stage, but specific and tangible enough to be meaningful and inspiring and to help remind you of what you want?

I find that the best way to create your vision board is to grab a bunch of magazines, cut out pictures and words or phrases that resonate with you, and stick them onto a big board or piece of paper that you can position in a prominent place. Put it up on your fridge, place it by your desk, or keep it in your pocket, so that you can keep looking at it and start working on getting closer to your vision.

This is not a case of creating a vision for what you want and then sitting back, expecting all your dreams to come true. But having a vivid idea of what it is that you want will help you stay focused on taking action to make it happen.

Exercise 1-1:

1. What are your reasons for escaping the 9 to 5?
    a. What are your *push* reasons – what are you escaping from?

      b. What are your *pull* reasons – what are you escaping to?

2. What is it you want to *do*? What is it you want to *be*? What is it you want to *have*?
3. What does your ideal day look like?
4. What if it all works out exactly as you hope?
5. Have a go at creating a vision board to bring this all to life.

IDENTIFYING YOUR CORE VALUES

Defining my personal values was one of the first exercises I did as I started my coach training, and it came as a bit of a surprise to me. I think I saw values as something connected to ethics or religion, preferring more tangible goals and objectives to focus my efforts. But I've found this such a valuable (!) exercise for myself and, over the years since, for my clients as well.

Understanding your values, having that clarity on what really matters to you, provides a framework to help guide your decisions. In the context of your business, it can help you choose the right business model, identify the type of clients you want to be working with, and set boundaries for how you're going to work – all things that we'll be looking at in this book.

You can see how different it is if my values are "home, family, generosity, harmony, humanity" versus if my values are "strength, excellence, professionalism, advancement, wealth". And, by the way, there is no judgement here. It's important that you choose the values that truly matter to you and don't worry about what others might think. You will come up with your own unique concoction that is meaningful to you.

Now, of course, you can Google lists of values, and I will share some examples below; but I prefer a more organic approach, where you first reflect spontaneously on what your values might be. Clients will also often ask me, "Is that a value? Or is it a strength? Is it a feeling? Is it a belief...?" And it doesn't really matter; that's just semantics. The point, as with all these exercises, is that it's something that you value, that's important to you, and that guides your decisions in a meaningful way.

The key is that you understand what the word means to you, and you 'double click' to dig into that deeper meaning. If I take 'creativity' as a value, for example, that might mean creating art or music, or it might be more about coming up with creative solutions or expressing yourself in a creative way. Make sure you're clear on what it means to you.

Examples of values: *Abundance, Advancement, Adventure, Affection, Appreciation, Authenticity, Balance, Beauty, Career, Caring, Change, Charisma, Clarity, Comfort, Communication, Compassion, Connection, Contentment, Contributing, Cooperation, Courage, Creativity, Diversity, Effectiveness, Endurance, Enjoyment, Excellence, Excitement, Faith, Fame, Family, Freedom, Friendship, Fun, Generosity, Goodness, Grace, Gratitude, Happiness, Harmony, Home, Honesty, Humanity, Humour, Independence, Innovation, Integrity, Intelligence, Involvement, Justice, Kindness, Knowledge, Leadership, Learning, Love, Loyalty, Openness, Order, Patience, Peace, Play, Power, Professionalism, Prosperity, Respect, Security, Self-respect, Spiritualism, Strength, Success, Wealth, Wellness, Wisdom*

Highs and lows

Perhaps you have a clear idea of what your values are already. Or maybe, like me, it's something that you've not really asked yourself before. How can you get clear on what really matters?

Well, one exercise that can help is to explore your 'lifeline' from your childhood right through to where you are today. Consider both the positive and the negative experiences that you've had so far and, most insightfully, what drove those experiences.

Figure 3: Your lifeline

When were you at your happiest, which were your happiest moments? When were you most proud of yourself? And when did you feel the most fulfilled?

What have been the highlights in your career, in your personal life, your hobbies, travels, sporting achievements, or family milestones? For me, they might include graduating as valedictorian (top of my high school class), being accepted to study at Oxford, getting a top rating in my first job, quitting my job (yes, it was one my happiest and proudest moments), and writing and publishing my first book. In my personal life, getting the lead role in a play in my amateur theatre group, road tripping with my aunt up the Californian coast, paddleboarding on the Mississippi River, meeting my partner and having our two children, and fulfilling a lifelong ambition to live by the sea.

What have been the low points? Professionally, they might include a terrible boss and toxic office culture, an experience of burnout, or being made redundant. Personally, maybe you had a tough breakup, ongoing marital problems, or an illness in the family?

Consider the most memorable and therefore most important milestones that have shaped you, as these will shed light on the moments when you were living in alignment with your values, and when there was a disconnect.

Finding the patterns

One of the first frameworks that I developed in my early coaching work was the 'guiding star'. This represents five different aspects of what is important to you, to help guide you in your career decisions: your core values; your 'desired feelings'; the environment in which you thrive; your personal strengths; and your characters.

As you explore the different moments on your 'lifeline', taking them individually and together, look for what they are telling you about what's important to you. What are the patterns? Specifically, ask yourself:

- **How were you feeling?**
- **What was the environment like?**
- **What strengths were you using (or not using)?**
- **Who were you being?**
- **What values were shining through?**

VALUES

CHARACTERS

FEELINGS

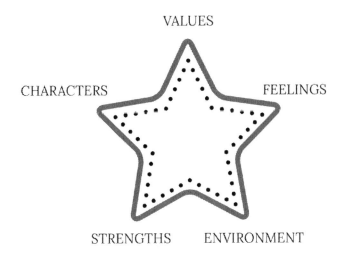

STRENGTHS   ENVIRONMENT

Figure 4: Your guiding star

Taking each point of the star in turn, let's start with your desired feelings. In the book, *The Desire Map* (2014), Danielle Laporte explains her concept of 'core desired feelings'. She talks about the masculine energy goals of, "I want to have a big house," "I want to live by the sea," "I want to be a best-selling author." These are your traditional goals, usually focused on a traditional definition of success. Instead, she prefers the more feminine energy of identifying how you want to feel. "I want to feel free," "I want to feel radiant," "I want to feel significant."

The example I always think of is, "I want to buy a big house." A standard, perfectly acceptable, goal. But why do you want that house? And why do you want to specifically buy it? Becoming a homeowner could give you security and safety; a sense of belonging and connection in your local community; and an opportunity to express yourself creatively through the interior design. On the other hand, it could make you feel trapped by all your obligations, with a mortgage to pay and all the house renovations and repairs that are inevitably needed, and you're not going to be as free to just pack up your things and go travelling.

Rather than setting yourself a goal to "buy a big house", it can be more meaningful to first understand how you want to feel. Do you long for that sense of safety, security, and belonging, or are you rather drawn to freedom and adventure? Even if you want security and belonging, there may be a different (and 'better') way of achieving it than necessarily having to buy that big house.

Consider the feelings that are associated with each of those different milestones on that 'lifeline'. What do you want more of? What do you want less of?

Examples of core desired feelings: Abundant, Adventurous, Aligned, Alive, Authentic, Blissful, Bold, Brave, Bright, Centred, Connected, Creative, Curious, Daring, Divine, Ecstatic, Effervescent, Elated, Electric, Energised, Engaged, Enthusiastic, Expansive, Feminine, Fierce, Flourishing, Flowing, Free, Full, Genuine, Glorious, Graceful, Harmonious, Heroic, Infinite, Intentional, Irresistible, Light-hearted, Luxurious, Magical, Masculine, Mindful, Nourished, Open, Passionate, Peaceful, Playful, Powerful, Precious, Present, Radiant, Real, Relaxed, Sacred, Safe, Self-assured, Sensuous, Serene, Sexy, Significant, Soulful, Still, Strong, Substantial, Supported, Tender, Tranquil, Unfiltered, Vibrant, Wide-eyed, Wild-hearted

The next point on the star is more straightforward: what's the environment in which you thrive? Reflecting on the highlights and lowlights on your lifeline, what was the environment in which you were operating at these pivotal moments in your life? Were you part of a team or working alone? Did you spend your days out and about, or were you sitting at your computer within a traditional office environment? Were you a small fish in a big company or a big fish in a small company? Was the organisation process-driven with clear roles and responsibilities, or was it more flexible and creative?

Examples of work environments: *Collaborative, Compassionate, Competitive, Connected, Creative, Data driven, Diverse, Efficient, Entrepreneurial, Fast-paced, Flexible, Formal, Harmonious, Hierarchical, Inclusive, Informal, Innovative, In-person, Isolated, Loud, Multi-cultural, Open, Organised, Process-driven, Professional, Respectful, Quiet, Social, Supportive, Traditional, Transparent, Trusting, Virtual, Warm*

The third point on the star is, what are your strengths? We'll dig into this more later but, for now, which strengths were you leveraging when you were at your best? What were the hard and soft skills that you were using and, more significantly, what were the personality strengths that you demonstrated?

Examples of personality strengths: *Action-oriented, Analytical, Artistic, Calm, Capable, Caring, Charming, Collaborative, Commanding, Communicative, Compassionate, Considerate, Cooperative, Courageous, Creative, Curious, Decisive, Dedicated, Dependable, Detail-oriented, Diligent, Diplomatic, Disciplined, Driven, Emotionally intelligent, Empathetic, Energetic, Entertaining, Fast, Flexible, Focused, Helpful, Independent, Inspiring, Intelligent, Level-headed, Loyal, Methodical, Meticulous, Observant, Optimistic, Organised, Outgoing, Patient, Positive, Precise, Reflective, Resilient, Resourceful, Responsible, Self-motivated, Sensitive, Strategic, Team-oriented, Thoughtful, Trustworthy, Visionary, Warm*

The fourth point of the star is, what are the different sides to your personality, the different characters, that need to be allowed to play out? For me, for example, there is a 'good girl' side, the prolific student who works hard and who has allowed me to attain so many of those academic and professional achievements. There's also a free-spirited hippie adventurer who loves to travel and explore the world. There is a nurturing mother who cares more than anything about her children. There is a confident and ambitious business owner who wants to make an impact in the world. There is a sensual woman who wants to feel attractive and experience romance and love.

If you shut a few of those characters out, and you focus only on one part of who you are, then you're not allowing yourself to show up as a whole person and, by extension, to be successful in a complete way.

The final point on the star represents your values, bringing us full circle to the start of the chapter. The beauty of designing your own business is that you can choose work and clients that reflect those values, leverage your strengths, and allow your different characters to come to the fore, while designing an environment that will support your goals and your desired feelings.

Exercise 2-1:

1. What values come to mind, spontaneously, for you?
2. What are the important milestones of your life?
    a. When were you the happiest? Most proud? Most fulfilled?
    b. When were you the least happy, proud, and fulfilled?
3. What patterns can you find in your different milestones?
    a. How did you feel?
    b. What was the environment?
    c. What strengths were you using (or not using)?
    d. Who were you being?
    e. What values are shining through?'

Narrow down your list to five values so that you have a list that's broad enough to be flexible, but specific enough to be useful.

DEFINING YOUR PURPOSE

The idea of your Purpose might sound idealistic, and it's true that it is a big word – it can be intimidating – and it is also a powerful one. There's a reason why it has become so ubiquitous, whether you're talking about 'starting with why', as Simon Sinek would say, creating a purpose-driven business, or finding the personal meaning of your life.

The fact that your purpose is 'big', however, doesn't mean that it needs to be scary and complicated to come up with. As Héctor García, co-author of *Ikigai: The Japanese secret to a long and happy life* (2017, p.183), puts it:

> *Life is not a problem to be solved. Just remember to have something that keeps you busy doing what you love, while being surrounded by the people who love you.*

So, yes, we are talking about your purpose and getting clear on what you want, and I'm giving you all sorts of prompts to come up with your vision; but we don't need to overcomplicate things. We don't have to come up with a pithy sentence, a formal Definition of Success – that's not what I'm asking you to do here, and it's certainly not what I've done myself. Your definition of success, and your purpose, can be as simple as doing work that you enjoy and spending time with the people you love.

In this context of finding your purpose, I've been exploring the concept of 'ikigai' for some years. It's a Japanese word that means something along the lines of the French 'raison d'être'. It's the thing that gives you joy, your reason for jumping out of bed in the morning, your drive; it's what will allow you to live a long and happy life.

You may have seen this concept represented in the form of a Venn diagram floating around on the internet. My understanding now is that astrologist Andrés Zuzunaga (2011) created an initial version of this in Spanish, where your *propósito* or purpose sits at the intersection of *lo que haces bien, lo que amas, lo que el mundo necesita*, and *por lo que te pagarán*. Marc Winn (2014) later combined this diagram with the Japanese concept of ikigai, and this has become the ubiquitous 'ikigai Venn diagram' that is often shared on social media.

Whether you call it your purpose or your ikigai, the core idea is valuable and resonates with a lot of us. I've adapted it slightly to help you get clear on what's important to you and, more specifically, to design the business that allows you to escape the 9 to 5.

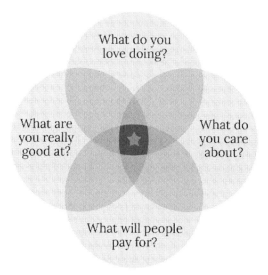

Figure 5: Finding your purpose

So, this business can be found at the intersection of four things:

- **What are you really good at?**
- **What do you love doing?**
- **What do you care about?**
- **What will people pay for?**

The first circle is your skills and your strengths – these are the things that you're good at. Often, you'll stop there, by the way, and you'll choose a business idea and a business model just because it's something that you can do. The fact that you *can* do it, however, doesn't necessarily mean that it's going be fulfilling, financially lucrative, or enjoyable.

The second circle is what you love doing – when you're in that flow and you don't even notice that time is passing because you're so 'in the zone'. Loving what you do means that you'll be more committed to the work and so you'll be more likely to get results. Of course, you're never going to be able to build a business on just the things you love doing, but the goal is to tip the balance in that direction.

The third circle is sometimes called 'what the world needs' but I like to consider the things that you care about. What's the impact, the difference, that you want to make in the world? What would be meaningful for you?

Finally, because it's a business and not a hobby or a charity, the fourth circle is what people will pay for. So, how might you monetise your ideas?

In the 'corporate 9 to 5', you might find yourself in the bottom left of the diagram. You're very good at what you are doing – because you've built a successful career in this area – and people are paying you well for that work. However, maybe you don't care about the product, it doesn't feel like you're doing something that is truly meaningful, and you don't exactly love it either.

Alternatively, if you are working in the charity sector and doing incredibly worthwhile work, but you are not getting paid so generously, then you might be in the top part of the diagram, missing the monetisation piece.

Ask yourself, where do you find yourself today? What's the biggest thing that's missing? Is it the passion for what you're doing that you're missing? Is it the enjoyment of your work? Is it that you do enjoy your work, but you're not earning enough? Knowing where you are, and where you want to get to, can help guide your decisions going forward.

Now, let's break these four areas down, one by one.

Mapping your skills and strengths

The first element is, what are you really good at? The tendency here is to look very narrowly and specifically at what you happen to be doing today, that is, your current job title. "I am a social media manager," "I am a digital marketing expert," "I am an HR director," and so on. That is part of it but, first, you will have had many different roles in your career and, second, and more importantly, within each of those roles, you will have done so much more than what the job title suggests.

Consider the hard skills that you've learned across all your different roles, both professionally, in your career, and in your personal life, maybe through an extracurricular club or in a volunteering capacity. Your hard skills tend to be more technical and specific to the role and its seniority; they can be taught and are easier to quantify.

Then you have your soft skills, which relate more to how you work. These skills are more transferrable and can be relevant and applicable in different roles and professions. For example, critical thinking and problem solving, leadership, public speaking, pitching, and negotiating, collaborating in a team, and so on.

Finally, you have your personality strengths. These are the things that come naturally to you, that people always come to you for help with, and that represent your unique flair.

It's these three things taken together – your hard skills, soft skills, and personality strengths – that give you a solid foundation of expertise and competencies and make you credible to potential clients while giving you the confidence that you can deliver what you say.

Within your corporate role, you can start with your 360-degree feedback process, whether formally or informally, to gather insights from your manager, your colleagues, and your team members. You can also ask people in your personal life, so consider speaking to friends, family, or even your partner.

There are many different tools available to help you get clarity on your skills and strengths. Here are a few of the most popular ones…

Myers Briggs – This gives you four 'tendencies', whether you're extroverted (E) or introverted (I), intuitive (N) or sensing (S), feeling (F) or thinking (T), and perceiving (P) or judging (J). I'm an ENFP – enthusiastic, energetic, and independent. There is an argument that there is no scientific basis to this, but my clients and I have always found it very insightful and certainly the resulting profile is spot on for me.

Enneagram – There are nine different 'types': 1 The Perfectionist, 2 The Helper, 3 The Achiever, 4 The Individualist, 5 The Investigator, 6 The Loyalist, 7 The Enthusiast, 8 The Challenger, 9 The Peacemaker. My type is 7 The Enthusiast – adventurous, doesn't want to be tied down, and tends to overexert themselves.

CliftonStrengths Assessment – This used to be called the StrengthsFinder and consists of 34 different themes, grouped into four domains – Strategic thinking, Relationship building, Influencing, Executing – that together "explain your talent DNA". Last time I did this, I got Learning, Ideation, Restorative, Individualisation, and Achiever, and I can see how these feed into the business that I'm running today.

DISC – There are four dimensions here, Dominance, Influence, Steadiness, Conscientiousness. My highest dimension is I-Influence, being enthusiastic, gregarious, and persuasive, among other things. Personally, I found this one less useful, but I know lots of people who find it very powerful as well.

Have a look at these tools – by all means, consider others as well – while taking them with a pinch of salt. Taking a test, any test, will never give you all the answers. This is just another piece of the puzzle, another little ingredient, another contribution to your understanding of who you are.

Finding your flow

The second circle in the purpose diagram is, what do you love doing? When you're answering this, again, consider your current job, consider previous roles, but also what you do outside of work – volunteering, hobbies, and other interests. What would you do at the weekend, if you had the chance, or while on holiday? When you have some spare time, what do you find yourself doing?

There is the fascinating idea of 'flow', as studied by Mihaly Csikszentmihalyi (2002), where you don't even notice time has passed. You're in your zone of genius, you love it so much that it doesn't even feel like work to you. What does that look like for you?

A few prompts to get you thinking beyond the obvious, and perhaps remembering long-lost desires… What did you want to be when you were younger? It's Sunday night and you're excited about Monday morning – what are you going to be doing? If you took a year off, how would you spend your time? If you could go to any conferences or events this year, what would they be about? Who are your role models, who do you envy? What are you doing when you feel the most passionate and inspired? What would you like to do more of? If you had an hour to spend however you wanted, what would you do? Incorporating work that you love into the core of your business is critical to enjoying that business.

Connecting with meaningful causes

The third circle is, what do you care about? What does the world need? What gives your work meaning? Is there some bigger mission that you believe in?

This could be big picture, in the sense of fighting climate change, reducing plastics and saving the oceans, improving children's rights or women's rights; the areas of diversity, equity, and inclusion, and environmental, social, and governance are certainly full of worthy causes. It could also be something on a smaller scale and a bit more prosaic or personal. The point, as ever, is that you're choosing something that's important to you.

What causes do you care about, globally, or locally? What frustrates or angers you? What problem do you think deserves more attention? What principle would you dare to stand up for? More reflectively, what would you want people to say about you at your funeral? What legacy do you want to pass on to your children and grandchildren?

Is there a particular audience that you have in mind? For example, do you really want to help parents who are struggling with a specific challenge? Do you want to help young students, new hires, or retirees? Are you drawn to working with clients from specific cultural backgrounds, those of a certain economic status, or people who are neurodivergent?

Consider your personal journey as well. My whole business came about because I navigated the escape from the 9 to 5 – I wrote about my experience, and people started approaching me for help. My personal journey gives me credibility, even without all the coaching experience that I now have and the formal training and learning that I've completed. That journey, through my own struggles and transformation, also drives me to help other people through the same transition. So, if you've had your own health journey, career change, or personal transformation, that can be valuable to tap into as well.

Finding ways to make money

The final circle is, what will people pay for? We'll get into this in more detail when we get to Pillar 3 as we consider the business model. But maybe you've already had ideas about what kind of business you'd like to run? Is there a problem where you believe you've come up with a solution that people will pay for?

What are the things that you know people have already paid for? For example, if you've been paid to do a piece of consulting, or to do a talk, there is obviously a demand for a paid service there. If you see that other people are being paid for a particular service, then that's also a sign that there is a viable market, and that people are willing to pay.

Once you've explored these four different circles separately, take a step back and look at them together. What patterns can you see? For example, which core activities appear both in what you're good at and in what you love doing? Can you see a way to leverage that expertise and passion in a way that taps into a problem you care about, and that people (whether individuals or companies) will pay for? What are the common themes? In my experience, a business that sits at the intersection of these four circles is one that has a very high chance of being viable in terms of sustaining the life and lifestyle that you want.

Exercise 1-3:

1. Where do you find yourself today on the purpose diagram? What's missing?
2. What are you good at?
3. What do you love doing?
4. What do you care about?
5. What will people pay for?
6. What patterns do you see? What are the common themes?

FINDING THE RIGHT BALANCE

For the final step of this first pillar, we're going to look at finding the right balance, something that is core to the concept of redefining success.

Arianna Huffington is someone I follow closely in this area. Known initially for having founded Huffington Post, she shifted her focus after experiencing burnout herself to found Thrive Global, with the mission to end the burnout epidemic. Huffington (2020) expresses the issue like this:

> *When we chase a flawed definition of success, the danger is not only that it takes us to a place that's not truly where we want to go, it's that, on the way, we're much more likely to miss the things that really do bring us happiness, and fulfilment, like connection, meaning and impact.*

This is about redefining what success looks like and looking beyond the more traditional metrics of success to the things that really matter. It's a case of 'the emperor's new clothes' for me because it seems so obvious and almost mundane; but it's so, so, powerful.

Through my own work in this area, I've come up with a model that helps you look beyond the usual narrow focus on being successful just in the work domain. My model represents the five areas that matter in your life, the 5Ls: Live, Love, Learn, Lead, Laugh. These are the five areas that I believe are fundamental to achieving a sense of balance in life.

Importantly, I'm not saying that we should be aiming for a 10 out of 10 on each of these five areas, all the time. There will naturally be ebbs and flows, and we can also make intentional choices to prioritise some areas over others, at least for a time. What I am saying is that I want you to elevate above and beyond just looking at work in terms of that corporate career ladder and achievement in the traditional sense, to consider these other areas as well.

So, what are these 5Ls?

- **LIVE** is your health and wellbeing.

- **LOVE** is relationships and belonging – not just romance, but also community and your professional relationships.
- **LEARN** is development and growth.
- **LEAD** is career and impact. Yes, career is there, of course, but it's not about climbing that career leader but rather doing meaningful work and feeling like you're making a difference.
- **LAUGH** is the joy, the laughter, the fun in life. This is the one that is most often neglected, but it's arguably the most important.

Where are you in each of these areas today? And where do you want to get to? Let's look at them each in turn.

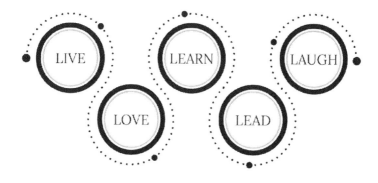

Figure 6: The 5Ls

LIVE – Health and wellbeing

First, what are your goals around wellbeing? Personally, I've made this a huge priority after having children, trying (insofar as it's possible) to get more sleep; making sure that I plan my runs and strength workouts first thing in the morning; getting my 10,000 steps a day; and so on.

I'm not a qualified nutritionist, personal trainer, or therapist, and I won't try to give you specific health advice here. I want to emphasise, however, that this is the basis for absolutely everything else; it really is the foundation of success. As I always say to my clients, "When you are your business, taking care of yourself is taking care of your business." If I burn out, if I get migraines, if I'm chronically unwell, then that has a direct impact on my business. We'll look at this again in Pillar 2, when we look at the importance of self-care.

LOVE – Relationships and belonging

What about your relationship goals? There is an element of romance here – so, if you're single, and you want to meet someone, that's important to think about (and that was me some years ago as I first embarked on my own career change). Although you'll often grab onto career change as an actionable solution, a pivotal moment in your life is usually not just about your work. These things tend to come hand in hand, and you don't just want to start a business, but you also want to meet someone, or start a family, or you need to get through a painful divorce at the same time.

Beyond love in the sense of romance, we're talking about your family, whatever that looks like for you – spending time with your children or your nieces and nephews, staying close to your brothers and sisters, making sure that you're maximising your time with your aging parents.

We're also looking at your professional relationships here, which are important too. So many people will feel lonely and isolated when they first quit their job to work for themselves if they haven't put in place the support structures or even the right business model (more on both later). There is a broader sense of belonging and community here that is a fundamental human need.

LEARN – Development and growth

Given that you're reading this book, I can safely say that you probably value lifelong learning as I do, and that will stand you in good stead as you develop your business. How are you looking to further learn and grow, personally and professionally?

What are you looking to learn in terms of how to run a business, in terms of the business itself? Maybe you need to upskill in a particular area? Maybe you want to develop your competence and confidence in a specific area such as public speaking, marketing, or sales? How will you continue to pursue professional development outside of the formal training opportunities that exists in a big company?

How are you looking to grow personally? Do you want to improve your relationship with your partner, grow in your role as a parent, or learn some other skill?

LEAD – Career and impact

What impact do you want to make in your work? This, of course, is what we're looking at throughout this whole book. What do you want to be doing in your work? What impact do you want to make? How are you looking to make a difference in your career?

LAUGH – Fun and spontaneity

Finally, what room are you leaving for fun and joy in your life? It can be harder to set goals in this rather vague and ephemeral area. Perhaps you want to leave some blank space in your diary for being spontaneous, for just having fun, and for expressing who you are. How can you make sure that you're nurturing yourself as a whole person while being a busy business owner?

Eve Rodsky (2022) calls this your 'unicorn space'. This area almost always gets deprioritised, unfortunately, and as Rodsky says, it should really come first.

Remember that the goal is not to get to a perfect 10 in each of the areas, and my intention here is not to give you more work to do on top of the business itself. I hope that this exercise opens your eyes to the different areas that need attention and that it prompts you to make even some small changes to get a better sense of balance in your life.

If you want to dig into these 5Ls in more detail, evaluate where you are today, and prioritise the right goals to get you to where you want to be, you can download a free assessment at onestepoutside.com/success.

Exercise 1-4:

1. What score would you give yourself in each of the areas today, where 1 is completely off track and 10 is spot on where you want to be?
    a. Live
    b. Love
    c. Learn
    d. Lead
    e. Laugh
2. Looking at your scores, where are the biggest gaps? Are you making an intentional choice to not make these areas a priority, or do you want to put more attention here?
3. What specific and meaningful goals do you want to set yourself in each of the areas (focusing on the ones with the biggest gaps versus where you want to be)?

Pillar 2:
Cultivating confidence & resilience

PILLAR 2:
CULTIVATING CONFIDENCE & RESILIENCE

Okay, so in Pillar 1, we've taken the time to reflect on the 'big picture' of what success means to you and what really matters. It's one thing, however, to have a big vision, or a big dream. It's another to truly believe that you can get there and to pick yourself up every time you – inevitably – experience disappointments, setbacks, and failures along the way.

Pillar 2 focuses on strengthening that belief in yourself and reframing the way you're thinking about things. This is about developing the resilience that you're going to need to cope with those ups and downs, to bounce back from any setbacks, and to set yourself up for success over the long haul.

We'll be looking, first, at identifying what we in coaching call your limiting beliefs. A lot of things that you take as fact are assumptions that you're making. You're seeing the world through a filter of your own life experiences and stories; they are not facts at all but rather beliefs. As you work towards realising your vision, if you find that these beliefs are holding you back, then it's important to reframe the way you're thinking and choose more empowering beliefs that will serve you and your goals. So that's the first step, identifying and reframing your limiting beliefs.

Next, we'll look at adopting a different kind of mindset. The mindset of being an entrepreneur, freelancer, solopreneur, business owner, whatever you want to call yourself – the mindset involved when you're working for yourself – is very different to the one you've been used to as an employee in a big corporation. We'll look at the kind of mindset that will support you in your endeavours outside of the 9 to 5, and how you can start making those shifts.

Then we're going to look at self-care. I know that this has become a bit of a cliché, but it is a cliché for a reason: when you are your business, taking care of you is taking care of your business. If you don't take care of yourself, well, first, that's not fun for you. It's certainly not good for you, or your family, and your general happiness and wellbeing. From a business point of view, as well, if your business lives and dies with you, then you really need to be fit and healthy to keep that business alive. So, we'll be looking at the different ways in which you can take care of yourself.

Finally, we'll look at the different types of support that you're going to need to get through this transition and make it sustainable for the long term. This journey through entrepreneurship can be isolating, and we don't want that to be the case for you. You've already picked up this book, which is a sign that you're open to learning and asking for help. We'll be looking at the different ways in which you can get all the support that you need.

So, let's get started with Pillar 2: cultivating your confidence and resilience.

REFRAMING YOUR LIMITING BELIEFS

The idea of limiting beliefs is a core coaching concept that doesn't necessarily come up in normal conversation but that can have a profound effect on how you're living your life and achieving your goals.

Whether you believe you can do a thing or not, you are right.
– Henry Ford

As with many of these inspirational quotes, it's disputed as to whether Henry Ford spoke these words; but the insight is important regardless. And I do think it's generally accepted, at least in theory – whether in sport, or in business, or in the entertainment industry – that you have to believe that you can do something in order to have a chance of doing it. Whether you're Richard Branson, or Usain Bolt, or Lady Gaga, you need to have had an extraordinary amount of self-belief to reach such lofty levels of success.

Conversely, there's an issue of possible self-sabotage that arises when you don't believe in yourself. You may have a really clear vision or set of goals – "This is what I want to do, I'm determined to make it happen, and I'm taking every action to do so" – and yet, subconsciously, you don't believe it's possible – "It's never going to happen, it's just a pipe dream, I'm not good enough."

It's important that you address this right away. I can give you all sorts of strategies, tools, and tactics. If, fundamentally, you don't believe that you're going to succeed, then you're simply not going to get the results that you want.

This holds true when you're just starting out and thinking about quitting a job to start your own business, taking that first leap. It's also true every day of working in your business, however many years in you are, because you need to keep believing as you keep building your business over the long term. It takes time to see results – I usually advise clients that it takes about three months to see the impact of the actions that you're taking today – and so there is a degree of faith needed in terms of expecting that things will work out as you keep putting in the effort without yet seeing the fruits of your labour.

Now, this doesn't mean that you can sit around waiting for things to happen for you; but having that sense of optimism and self-belief is critical alongside the actions that you're taking.

So where do these limiting beliefs come from? Well, they have usually developed out of a particular set of circumstances in your life. Your parents have told you stories, you've had your own experiences, or you've learned things from school, from society, from TV, and so on. These individual experiences are internalised and form in your head into stories, assumptions, and beliefs about what is and isn't possible. The stories might be about you and what you're capable of; they might be in relation to money; they might be around business and careers; and so on.

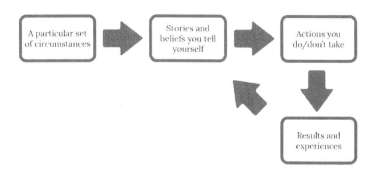

Figure 7: Where do limiting beliefs come from?

These beliefs that you hold will inform the actions that you do or don't take. So, if I'm told at school that, "you'll never make it as a writer, it's far too competitive," or "being a professional actress is a ridiculous pipe dream," then this will affect whether, and how, I pursue those ambitions. I'm probably not going to take my dreams of being an actress seriously and so I'm not going to apply to drama schools, or attend any auditions, or move to Hollywood to try and make it in the film industry. I'm going to be put off from pursuing my passion of writing as a full-time career and instead I'm going to go after a more 'sensible' profession.

I don't take the actions that would make the dream more likely (or even remotely possible). And, of course, what happens? Well, I won't be a famous actress, or an award-winning journalist, because I haven't even tried to realise those ambitions. If I haven't taken action, the belief that I won't succeed becomes a self-fulfilling prophecy and I can say with certainty that I'm not going to make it.

Now, I did end up doing a lot of drama in my last couple of years at school, and later found an amateur theatre and musical group where I was very active alongside my full-time marketing job. And, really, being a Hollywood actress was never a meaningful goal for me. When it comes to the writing piece, for many years, I completed a range of creative writing courses as well as a journalistic diploma alongside my work; I've written many an article for my own blog as well as for online and offline publications; and, hey, here I am, writing a book. But it has taken years for me to bring that dusty dream down from the shelf and take it seriously.

Let's take an example that is more directly related to this process of escaping the 9 to 5. If you tell yourself, and others, that you want to quit your job to work for yourself, but you fundamentally believe that "I will never succeed as an entrepreneur," "I won't make enough money," "I can't charge X amount for that service," and so on... What happens? Well, you won't take the leap to work for yourself as you don't think it will be viable; you subconsciously limit yourself when it comes to how much you can earn; you don't raise your prices, or you show up feebly on a sales call to the point that the prospective client can't help but reinforce your belief that they aren't willing to invest at that level. It becomes a vicious cycle where you yourself are making the very outcome that you fear inevitable. This is the cycle that you need to break.

Now, a lot of these beliefs have come about, again, because of a particular set of circumstances and experiences. This means that they have, at one point, been true for you, and that they have served a purpose in your life in the past. The key question for you now is: do they still serve you today? Will holding onto these beliefs support your current vision and objectives?

There is an innate human drive in you to keep yourself safe at all costs. Your beliefs are designed to support that survival instinct, keeping you from taking risks that will threaten you and your safety. While that may have been helpful in a world of sabre-toothed tigers and rival tribes, it's not so helpful in the modern-day world. Keeping you 'safe' now means keeping you in a comfort zone where you won't go after your biggest dreams and desires, you'll stick to what you know, and you'll avoid anything that risks you making a mistake or looking foolish.

Identifying your limiting beliefs

The first step in trying to break the vicious cycle is to identify your limiting beliefs. Again, you might think that these are facts, but that is precisely the issue. You take your world view as based on universal truths; but your so-called truths are very different to my truths because your experiences, your parents, your upbringing, as well as your innate personality, are all different to mine.

If you have entrepreneurial parents, they will have certain assumptions themselves, based on their own experiences, that they will pass onto you – both directly and indirectly. If they've been successful entrepreneurs, then that will colour your experience and bolster your belief that you can be a successful entrepreneur. On the other hand, if they've struggled, or they never had time for you when you were younger because they were working so hard, then that affects you in a different way. If your parents had high-flying corporate jobs, if they were academics, if they were artists; and if they were happy and fulfilled, stressed and over-worked, or if they were unemployed... these things will all affect how you view different career paths and possibilities.

To makes this more tangible, let's look at some examples, which I imagine may sound familiar.

"Working for yourself is riskier than having a job."
There is a prevalent belief, which often isn't even voiced, that working for yourself means that you don't have a stable salary, pension, and other benefits that come with being an employee, and that this makes being your own boss inherently risky.

"It's irresponsible to go after what I want."
I get this a lot from clients, when they caveat any dream that they've dared to express with, "Oh, but, you know, it's very idealistic of me..." They might be clear on what they truly want to do, but they tell themselves that it's not just risky but completely reckless to try to go after it.

"Work isn't supposed to be fun; it's just supposed to pay the bills."
This is the Protestant work ethic talking; hard work is your duty. "Work is work; it's supposed to be painful." "Who am I to think that I should enjoy my work?" "I should be grateful that I have this well-paying job." And so on.

"You have to choose between money and fulfilment."
This is a real bugbear for me and is typical of the black-and-white thinking that we often resort to. "You can't be creative and earn a good living." "You can either pursue your purpose or you can have a well-paid job." This kind of thinking manifests in the overall decision as to which career or business to pursue and then it reappears when it comes to specific strategic decisions. "I can either work with corporate clients who will pay me lots of money, or I can do more fulfilling work with individuals but accept that I'll earn less."

"I'm not entrepreneurial at all; I'm not good enough…"
These are beliefs about your own skills and strengths, your identity, and what you're capable of. There's an assumption that business owners are a special kind of unicorn born with an entrepreneurial gene that the rest of us can't learn.

"It may work for other people, but it won't work for me because of X, Y, Z reasons."
Again, there are unicorns in the world; people are luckier, or better, or just different. They don't have all the limitations that you do – limited time, money, a young family… – and that's why they have been able to be successful. "It might be possible for them, but it will never work for me."

Reframing your beliefs

Even just putting these beliefs down on paper is a valuable exercise. Once you have articulated them, you can examine them in more detail. Taking each one in turn, you can ask yourself:

- **Is it a helpful belief? Is it serving you and the goals that you have today?**
- **Is it true?**
- **What would be a more empowering belief?**

Your answer to that first question might be, "yes, it is serving me – to some extent." As an example, if you take the belief that "having the stable salary of an employee is really important," then this is serving you. It is helpful, in the sense that you need to be able to make a living, to feel secure in having a regular income, so that you can pay your bills and take care of yourself and your family. The belief has a role to play in keeping you and your family safe.

However, does the part on having to be an employee to get that salary serve you? If you're stuck in a job or career where you are fed up with the bureaucracy of a big corporation, feeling unfulfilled from doing work that isn't meaningful to you, and burning out from the long hours and poor work-life balance… does believing that you have to stay in a job, and in that job in particular, serve you? Is it helpful for you now, as you look towards a different vision for yourself that involves putting your own wellbeing, time with family, and fulfilment first?

Second, if it's not helpful, ask yourself, "is it true?" You will have formed this belief based on experiences and lessons you've learned in the past; however, if you open your eyes and start looking for new data points, you will most often be surprised by the amount of evidence that you find to the contrary. In fact, you'll always find evidence to support your existing world view, as you filter everything through a particular lens; so, why not choose a lens that will support you and your vision?

And then, "What would be a more empowering belief?" Because, yes, it may surprise you, but you can choose your beliefs. Once you've chosen a belief, you can open your eyes, filter for those positive experiences, and look for people and stories that support that new belief.

When I first left my job, my whole interview series with people who escaped the 9 to 5 – which started off on the blog, became the *Leaving the Corporate 9 to 5* book, and now continues on the Reimagining Success™ podcast – came about precisely because of this. I was looking for inspiring stories from other people who had 'done it', and that opened my eyes to the possibility that, "Hey, this really is possible."

Likewise, the sabbatical I took to travel across South America before quitting my job in 2013 opened my eyes to a whole world of new experiences. I left my little bubble in Geneva and met people living very different lives while making very different career and lifestyle choices. Along the way, I collected evidence of all the incredible things that were possible that I hadn't considered.

Let's go back to the previous set of examples and see how you might reframe them.

"Working for yourself is riskier than having a job."

- First, is it a helpful belief? "No, it's not helpful right now, because I want to work for myself."
- Secondly, is it true? "No, it's not true. The 'security' of being in a job is false. We're not in control of our own destiny; there may be mergers and acquisitions, and redundancies; as we near retirement, we can face discrimination. Working for yourself may, in fact, be less risky as you can diversify your income streams and you are in control of what you are doing and how much you are earning."
- Finally, what is a more empowering belief? "I choose instead to believe that working for myself gives me more security than being an employee."

"It's irresponsible to go after what I want."

- Is this a helpful belief? "No, because it's keeping me from going after my most important goals."
- Is it true? "No, it's not irresponsible. Working on my goals will inherently bring me more happiness and fulfilment; I'll make a bigger impact in the world as I follow my passion and purpose; and I will be a good role model for my children."
- What is a more helpful belief? "It's important that I go after what I want, while sensibly managing the risk."

"Work isn't supposed to be fun."

- Is it helpful? "Nope, it's making me miserable."
- Is it true? "No, I know a lot of people who enjoy their work."
- New belief? "Work can, and should be, fun."

"You have to choose between money and fulfilment."

- Helpful? "No, because it means that I can either have a comfortable lifestyle with a high-paying job, or I can do meaningful and fulfilling work, but I can't have both."

- True? "No. A lot of people do fulfilling work and earn a comfortable living doing so."
- New belief? "It's absolutely possible to earn a good living doing fulfilling work; in fact, finding work that I'm passionate about will mean that I'll happily work harder, make more of a difference, and therefore be more likely to earn more money."

"I'm not entrepreneurial; I'm not good enough."

- Helpful? "No, because I want to work for myself, and this poor self-belief is preventing me from fulfilling that ambition."
- True? "Not at all. 'Good enough' for whom? I may not know how to do certain things *yet* but I can learn."
- New belief? "There's no such thing as being born 'entrepreneurial' and I can and will learn whatever is necessary."

"It may work for others, but not for me."

- Helpful? "No, I'm just envious of others who are out there doing what I want to be doing."
- True? "The truth is that everyone faces limitations; everyone has the same number of hours in the day, and if someone else has achieved success it's because they have put in the effort to overcome those obstacles and achieve their success in spite of personal challenges."
- New belief? "Everyone has challenges, and I will find a way to overcome mine."

Exercise 2-1:

1. List all the beliefs you have around work, career, entrepreneurship, money, as well as family, work-life

balance – anything that relates to designing this life and business outside of the 9 to 5.

2. For each of these beliefs, ask yourself: (i) is it helpful? and (ii) is it true?

3. Have a go at reframing each of your limiting beliefs into a more empowering one that serves your goals. Then, look for evidence to support that new belief. You might find that evidence in my book, *Leaving the Corporate 9 to 5*, or in my 'Escaping the 9 to 5' Facebook community; you might find it at events where you'll meet inspiring role models; you'll certainly find it as you start broadening your circle and working on your new business.

EMBRACING A DIFFERENT MINDSET

One of my mum's favourite stories from my childhood, which is very fitting in this context of confidence and resilience, is about Helen Keller, the American disability rights advocate and political activist. There was a project at primary school – and forgive me for this little side note – over half-term where I had to write about Helen Keller…

Just as we were leaving school for half-term, I met one of my best friends who told me that the project was due right after the break. Instead of checking this with the teacher – especially because I had thought the deadline was later – I then spent the whole week "hustling away" as we'd call it now, working late into the night on this project. We only had a Swedish book at home on Helen Keller, so a lot of time was spent first translating key elements into English.

When we came back to school after our break, it turned out that the deadline was, indeed, later – and, funnily enough, my friend had not spent her holiday working on it. You could take this whole experience as an example of my not having taken responsibility for my homework deadlines. Instead, my mum generously refers to this incident as an example of my grit, working relentlessly to get the job done.

Helen Keller, therefore, has a special place in my heart. I've recently discovered the following quote from this inspiring individual (Keller, 2010):

> *Optimism is the faith that leads to achievement; nothing can be done without hope.*

Optimism often gets a bad rap, associated as it is with being overly idealistic and naive; here, Keller suggests that you need to have that faith, hope, and confidence in yourself and in the world if you're ever to succeed in your endeavours. If you're pessimistic instead, you'll never try anything, you'll never believe that you will succeed, and so why bother?

This is important. Optimism is a key element of resilience, which is what's going to get you through the highs and lows.

Of course, it's easier said than done, but already beginning to think this way will help when it comes to your mindset.

There is an enduring metaphor of a rollercoaster ride through the inevitable ups and downs of managing your own business. Wherever you are on this journey, whether right at the beginning or somewhere in the middle, this image is probably at the forefront of your mind as a fear, or as the reality, of what it feels like to work for yourself.

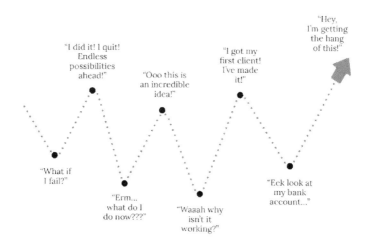

Figure 8: The rollercoaster of escaping the 9 to 5

When you're first thinking of starting a new endeavour – in this case, quitting your job to start your own business – you'll likely be filled with doubts and those limiting beliefs that we've just looked at. "What could I possibly do after all these years in the same career?" "What if I fail??" "I have no idea where to start!"

If you can overcome those initial fears, if you have the courage to take the leap, then you do quit your job. You have this amazing moment of freedom and empowerment, where others tell you, "Wow, you're so lucky!" "You're so brave!" and the whole world is full of promise and opportunities.

Then, suddenly, your days stretch out in front of you. You begin to ask yourself, "What am I supposed to do with this time? Where should I be focusing?" "Oh my goodness! What have I done?!" "Have I made a mistake?"

Then you have an incredible idea that gets you excited, "This is amazing! This is going to be so good!"

And then when things inevitably take longer than you thought, "Why isn't it working?" You succumb to the temptation to check job postings and maybe even send out a few scattergun applications as you think you might have to go back to full-time employment.

Suddenly something clicks. "I got my first client! I'm getting paid! It's working!!"

But it's only the beginning and "Gaaah my bank balance is dropping; I'm spending all my savings…"

Then, as things continue to progress, the results start coming in, and you build your confidence as you think, "Hey, I'm getting the hang of this!"

Over time, if you stick with it, there will be more and more highs and, above all, you'll be better equipped to deal with the lows. You'll have a solid business plan, along with more confidence and credibility, and you will have developed your resilience.

But the truth is that the rollercoaster never fully goes away, even after years of building your business. That's why having a support system, working on your mindset, reframing your beliefs – everything that we're looking at in this second pillar – is so critical.

Adopting a growth mindset

We've looked at the importance of an optimistic outlook. Next, I want to introduce a concept from Carol Dweck. In her appropriately named book *Mindset* (2017), Dweck draws the distinction between having a growth mindset, which will support your success, and having a fixed mindset, which will limit you and hold you back.

A traditional education, at least in my personal experience, teaches you to have a fixed mindset. You're either a whizz with numbers or you hate maths and find it difficult; you're a natural linguist or you're no good at languages; you're sporty or you're not, you're a good writer or you're terrible. Whatever the subject, you're labelled 'good' or 'not good'. This approach represents a fixed mindset where there's no point in trying when something is hard, because you're just not good at this thing and you never will be. Here you can recognise those limiting beliefs coming into play again.

Dweck's growth mindset, on the other hand, is more constructive and optimistic. A student with a growth mindset won't give up. They will ask, "How can I work this out? How can I come up with a creative solution? I may not know the answer yet, but I will find out."

Let's first explore what a fixed mindset looks like. See if you recognise yourself any of these types of statements.

- "I'm just not good at [fill in the blank here]." (For example, sales, marketing, finance...)
- "It's too hard. There's no point in trying. I'll never manage."
- "Oh, no, I failed. I might as well give up now."
- "I'll never be as good as that person over there."
- "I'm going to stick with what I know and not try anything new."

Next, what does a growth mindset look like?

- "I can't do this yet because I haven't done it before. So of course, it's new to me – but I'm going to learn."
- "This is challenging, but I'm going to grow from this experience and emerge stronger as a result."
- "What can I learn from this so-called failure or setback, so I can get a better result next time?

- "Okay, that person over there is doing really well – what can I learn from them and how can I be inspired by their success?"
- "I'm willing to try new things, because that's what will get me results."

Do you recognise yourself in the statements from the fixed mindset, or rather the growth mindset? If you find yourself more in the fixed mindset, see how you can start making that shift towards a more empowering growth mindset.

- How can you look for opportunities to stretch yourself and take on bigger challenges so that you grow with them?
- When you come up against an obstacle, how can you resolve to find a solution and see any failure along the way as an opportunity to learn?
- How can you start to view effort as the necessary path to mastery?
- Instead of ignoring criticism, or taking it personally, how can you see it as a source of valuable information to help you do better next time?
- Rather than feel threatened by other people's successes, how can you use them as inspiration?

It takes time to shift the way your mind works. Start by becoming aware of your fixed mindset whenever it rears its head, and then try to shake things up as you focus on opportunities to learn and grow.

Getting out of your comfort zone

Speaking of stretching yourself… If you flip back to the spine of this book, you'll see the logo, One Step Outside™. This is the name of my coaching and mentoring business (and my publishing house if you want to get fancy about it). It comes from an unattributed quote, that "Everything you've ever wanted is *one step outside* your comfort zone."

This idea of the growth that comes from challenging yourself and getting uncomfortable is a concept that I've had at the core of my coaching ever since I first started my training. As part of my certification with the ICF-accredited International Coach Academy, I developed what we called a "power tool" that pitted 'growth' against 'comfort'. In fact, my whole coaching model was built around this idea of getting out of your comfort zone and it is still an important part of the work that I do personally as well as how I help my clients.

There is a comfort zone where you feel safe and secure. Again, we come back to that prehistoric survival instinct that protects you from the sabre-toothed tiger. It's not as helpful these days; but there are still benefits that come from staying safe. There are valid reasons why you're holding on to the familiar and staying in your comfort zone, and it's important to recognise this and show yourself some compassion and understanding.

If you imagine a set of concentric circles. Right in the middle, you have your comfort zone – this is where you feel safe and secure. You have a routine, and you know exactly what you're doing. You've got the prestige, the status, and respect of your peers. Outside of that first circle, there's a second circle, which is your growth zone. This is where you're going to challenge yourself, learn new things, and grow in confidence along the way.

Fear will keep you in your comfort zone; courage is what helps you step out and into your growth zone. The fear will never go away completely and, as I always say, 'scary' tends to come along for the ride with anything that is also 'exciting'. Note that you don't have to take a massive leap here – you can absolutely take a small step and that is, of course, the 'one step outside'.

Although there is an element of fear in the growth zone, there's a world outside of the growth zone that you might call the panic zone. If you do too much too soon, then that's where you'll end up, flying a bit too free. That's when 'exciting' and 'exhilarating' become 'terrifying' and 'debilitating' and that's not a good place to be.

It's important not to go too big too soon, because that's when you panic; that's when you try to speak to recruiters and try to get another job again. That's when you withdraw back into your comfort zone, only to lose sight of all those incredible goals that you had and lose the progress that you have made. Know your limits; but keep forging ahead with those small steps.

Figure 9: Getting out of your comfort zone

As you step outside of your comfort zone and your confidence grows, you'll expand your old comfort zone to include this new thing that you've now experienced. Things that you previously saw as scary become part of your comfort zone, and you instead set your sights on something new and exciting. If you don't ever get out of your comfort zone, on the other hand, then that's when your comfort zone starts shrinking around you. This naturally happens with age if you don't keep pushing those boundaries and trying new things.

Exercise 2-2:

1. Where do you have an opportunity to work on developing more of a growth mindset?
2. What are the things that you don't know, or can't do, *yet* – and need to, or want to, learn?
3. What are the things that are outside of your comfort zone that you need to, or want to, find the courage to do anyway?

PRIORITISING SELF-CARE

Self-care is one of those overused words, a little cheesy – familiar from all those Instagram posts on #selfcare – but, as ever, it's a cliché for a reason. It's incredibly important; "self-care," as you may have seen in another social media meme, "is not selfish." Again, when you are your business, taking care of you is taking care of your business.

To deal with the inevitable ups and downs, the rollercoaster experience of especially those first weeks, months, and even years of working for yourself, you need to be taking care of yourself, first and foremost. It's so basic, and yet so easily forgotten, that you need to be healthy and rested so you have the energy and focus to do what you need to, and want to, do.

There will be ups and downs even when it comes to your wellbeing. You will be ill at some point, whether it's a simple cold, which can already feel debilitating, or a chronic illness that shows up in a more lasting way. At that point, it's even more important to take care of yourself as a priority.

What happens if you don't take care of yourself, and if you're not able to show up for your clients and your business (not to mention your family)? This is a little bit the fear as well, when it's just you as a solopreneur, when you're the only person working in the business and delivering a service. If you're unwell, then you can't take the client call, or deliver the workshop, or whatever it is that you've committed to doing. So, it's also important to develop a business model where you have the flexibility so that, if worse comes to worst, you can manage that as well.

The different levels of wellbeing

Not only is it easy to neglect your wellbeing altogether; it's also easy to over-simplify and think, "yeah, yeah, I know, I need a bit more sleep," or "I need to get more exercise." While those things are important, true wellbeing is so much more.

You're most likely familiar with Maslow's hierarchy of needs, represented in a pyramid. At the bottom, you have your physiological needs – air, water, food, shelter, sleep; next, you have your safety needs – personal security, employment, health; in the middle, you have love and belonging – friendship, intimacy, family; next, there is esteem – respect, status, recognition; and, finally, right at the top, you have self-actualisation – your desire to become the best that you can be.

Reflecting those same levels and applying it to your wellbeing specifically, I came up with the following:

- **your physical wellbeing;**
- **your mental wellbeing;**
- **your emotional wellbeing;**
- **your psychological wellbeing; and**
- **your spiritual wellbeing.**

It might seem like I'm over-intellectualising, but the intention is to get you thinking more holistically about your wellbeing.

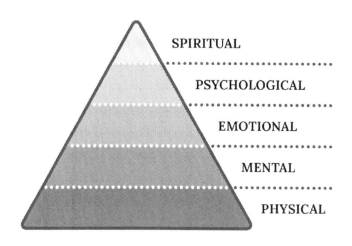

Figure 10: The 5 levels of wellbeing

Physical wellbeing

Taking each of these 'levels' of wellbeing in turn, let's start with the first one: how can you improve your physical wellbeing?

I'm not a doctor, a personal trainer, or a nutritionist, and that's not what I'm here to teach you. However, your physical wellbeing includes getting enough sleep – something that I've become painfully aware of as a mother of young children. Improving your sleep (within the realms of what's possible in your family situation) might involve trying to go to bed earlier and maybe having a nightly ritual, a bath, a chamomile tea… Your physical wellbeing also requires drinking plenty of water, eating nutritious food, exercising regularly… So how can you nurture your physical wellbeing?

If, like me, you spend most of your working day sitting at your desk, hunched over a computer…. Is it about getting up and stretching? Making sure that you take a five-minute break once an hour? What about trying a standing desk? What practical strategies can you adopt to improve your physical wellbeing?

You may find that need help with achieving your goals in this area. Last year, I worked with a nutritionist and coach who specialised in post-partum mothers; and then, once I had the basics in place, I worked with a personal trainer and coach who helped me dial up the exercise routine, lose the excess weight, and get back my energy and fitness. Although we all know, in theory, what we need to do, it's so much easier to hit our goals when we partner with someone who gives us tailored support and accountability.

Mental wellbeing

Second, what can you do to take care of your mental wellbeing? Thankfully, mental health is something that we're bringing much more focus to as a society and there's far less stigma attached to it than there was before. In a knowledge economy and a service-based business, your mind is doing all the hard work in your business. You need the headspace to deliver the work that you want to deliver to the standard that you desire.

What strategies do you need to nurture your mental wellbeing? Are you taking regular breaks, turning off your phone notifications, maybe having a bit of a digital detox away from social media now and again? There is an element of asking for help here as well. Do you have trusted friends and advisers who you can speak to? Do you want to see a therapist to talk things through? Your mental wellbeing is almost as foundational as your physical wellbeing.

Emotional wellbeing

Third, what can you do to take care of your emotional wellbeing? We're talking community, belonging, and feeling that you're a part of something bigger than yourself. What can you do to nurture your relationship with your partner, with your family (whatever that looks like), and with your peers and colleagues?

Are you in my Escaping the 9 to 5 Facebook group, where you'll meet others who are going through the same career transition as you? Can you join, or even set up, a mastermind where you're part of a group of likeminded people who will 'get' what you're experiencing and help you feel less alone? Do you have friends and family members who are supporting you, cheering you on? What can you do to really support yourself emotionally?

Psychological wellbeing

Fourth, how can you take care of your psychological wellbeing? This, for me, goes beyond the basic mental state of managing stress, focusing effectively and being productive. This is about creativity, learning, intellectual stimulation, confidence, big picture thinking... It's all those things that you don't have time for when you're just running around being 'busy'.

What can you do to make time, create that space, free your mind, to dream of bigger things, envision the future, and find unexpected ideas and solutions to any problems you're up against? How can you allow for the expression of your creativity, to make room for innovative thinking, and make effective strategic decisions?

Spiritual wellbeing

Finally, and at the highest level, there is what you might call your spirit or soul. Irrespective of any religion, what can you do to nurture this deeper, or higher, level of wellbeing?

Would meditation help you stay more present and connected? Going to church? Spending time alone in nature? What about dancing, reading, or painting? What can you do to nurture this higher level and fulfil your highest potential?

Nourishing the different levels of wellbeing

There's no magical formula here, no blueprint to follow. I'm also not suggesting that you now add to your already far-too-busy schedule and commit to a long list of new habits in each area. Instead, my intention is to ask you some open-ended questions and offer you suggestions as to strategies you might consider if you feel one of these areas to be lacking. Maybe pick one area to start with, and one or two little changes or micro-habits to commit to, and then you can layer them on as you go.

Try to think in concrete terms here as to what changes you can make and how you can set yourself up for success. Can you have a big bottle that you fill up every morning and keep at your desk as an easy reminder to drink plenty of water throughout the day? Do you need to block your calendar to make sure that you take a proper lunch break? How about that classic trick, which really does work, of putting out your running shoes by the door the night before so that it's easy to get up and go first thing in the morning?

The key point here is that self-care, taking care of yourself, is not just about making some changes to your diet and exercise. Try to think about it in a more holistic way and consider the different things that go into feeling well in every sense of the word.

Do you feel isolated, working alone in your business? If you feel that you're struggling without a team around you, then finding that sense of community and belonging will be important. If you're living far away from your friends and family, if you're working from home all week, if you're feeling lonely – then your emotional wellbeing will be a priority.

If you've been sleeping badly, eating lots of sugar, drinking too much coffee, and generally neglecting your physical health, maybe there's an opportunity here to work with someone like a nutritionist or a personal trainer.

Think about where the gaps are for you, and what habits and rituals you can put in place to take care of those different aspects of your wellbeing.

Again, this is so critical. Your wellbeing really is the most important foundation for everything else in your life. If you're not well, how on earth can you expect to have a successful business? How will you be able take care of your kids, or be present with your partner? How can you enjoy life to its fullest?

A quick anecdote here, again, from my story-telling mother, this time about my dad. Mr Lundberg was the Director General of an international organisation, and then the CEO when it was privatised. He was at the very top of the company, and, indeed, of the industry. On this occasion, he wasn't very well. Of course, he couldn't possibly not go to this big upcoming meeting because he was so important, so critical to the business, and he'd be letting everyone down. So along he went, and what happened? He got pneumonia and was off work for two months. So then, the company had to do without him for two months.

Instead of taking care of himself at the beginning, and maybe having a shorter recovery, my dad foolishly and, I'd say, a little arrogantly, thought that "they can't possibly cope without me," and so he pushed, pushed, pushed; until he couldn't. (I say "arrogantly" with love and with the recognition that I think we're all quite arrogant in believing ourselves to be indispensable.)

And that's exactly what you don't want to do. You don't want to push, push, push until you burn out. You may well have experienced this already in your corporate role, and that may even be why you're now looking to build your own business. The lesson is clear: take a break and take care of yourself – before it's too late. And, again, there's an element of choosing and building the business model that will allow your business to survive a short illness which, let's face it, is inevitable at some point. We'll look at the business model in Pillar 3.

Exercise 2-3:

1. Where are the biggest gaps for you? Where do you want to focus? And what habits or rituals do you want to put in place? Consider:
   a. your physical wellbeing;
   b. your mental wellbeing;
   c. your emotional wellbeing;
   d. your psychological wellbeing; and
   e. your spiritual wellbeing.

CREATING A SUPPORT SYSTEM

And so, we come to the final piece of the second pillar, which is creating a support system. We've danced around this already in the past few chapters, and it really is key to setting yourself up for success.

Working for yourself doesn't mean that you're working in isolation. Please don't think that you have to do it, or even that you can do it, all by yourself. Maybe you could do it all alone, eventually, but I can promise you that it will be faster and more fun if you get the right support in place around you.

The fact that you're here reading this book means that you've already recognised the benefit of getting the right support from the right people. Indeed, there are a few different sources of support that you're going to need, not just at the start of your journey but throughout, as you level up and face different opportunities and challenges along the way.

For this one, I turn to President Barack Obama (2009):

> *Asking for help is not a sign of weakness, it's a sign of strength. It shows you have the courage to admit when you don't know something, and to learn something new.*

If Obama needs help, and can ask for help, then certainly the rest of us need it, and it's okay for us to ask for it as well.

This ties together a lot of the things that we've been talking about in this pillar, all about cultivating your confidence and resilience. The courage to get out of your comfort zone; the growth mindset to try something new and to recognise what you don't know; and now, the maturity and self-awareness to put aside your ego and ask for help.

So, what types of support do you need? For this one, I will highlight five areas: Accountability; Belief; Community; Disconnecting; and Expertise. So, let's talk through each of these, to give you an indication of the different aspects that are important when it comes to getting support.

Figure 11: What types of support do you need?

Accountability

The first type of support is accountability. I'm sure you've had the experience of enthusiastically setting yourself a goal, and then doing very little to achieve it.

Now, if you're very disciplined at sticking to your goals, and you have a strong sense of internal motivation and accountability – which is absolutely something that we can develop – then good for you, you can move onto the next type of support. The rest of us, however, need a little bit of help in holding ourselves accountable.

Accountability might involve making a public commitment, an announcement, so that others will remind you (and give you a hard time if you renege); having your partner's buy-in and support in helping you stick to your goals; or finding an accountability partner who's going through a similar process, whether it's in a fitness group or a business mastermind.

Having a coach is also powerful here. The simple act of booking your coaching call in the diary will implicitly mean that you're more inclined to do the work and keep taking action in between the calls. More concretely, you can also ask your coach to hold you accountable or, better yet, support you in holding yourself to account (which is subtly different but even more powerful than relying on external accountability in the long term). So, who's going to hold you accountable to your goals?

Belief

Secondly, who is going to believe in you? We've talked about your own beliefs and self-belief; but you also need those people in your life who say, "You're amazing! You can do it!" These are the people who will have unshakeable belief in your capabilities and cheer you on unconditionally.

It may be that the most obvious people in your life, the ones who are closest to you, are not the people who will provide this type of support early on. Not because they don't want to, but because they will project their own fears and insecurities onto you, which in turn will reinforce the same fears and insecurities that you are already experiencing. When you are working on addressing your limiting beliefs, you don't need others with that same old mindset to reinforce those beliefs that you're trying to replace.

Instead, you want to surround yourself with the people who will say, "Of course you can do it!" Often, these will be people who have done it themselves, which, by definition, means that they believe that you can do it too. As a result, you will be inspired by their success and start to believe in your own as well. If you're lucky, this could be a very supportive partner or a good friend; more likely, however, it might rather be a peer or colleague, or, again, a coach whose job it is to wholeheartedly support and believe in you.

Community

What communities are you part of? As we saw in the previous chapter, this is an important part of your emotional wellbeing, and it will also be an important part of your professional success.

I remember one of the first events I ever went to, back in 2013, which was a talk by a career coach. While I don't recall who she was or what she talked about, what I do remember is the strong sense of relief and reassurance that came from meeting others who were having the same thoughts and feelings about wanting to leave their corporate roles. I wasn't alone.

You can join my free community in the Escaping the 9 to 5 Facebook group or become part of the more intimate community of one of my paid programmes. There may also be local communities, where you can meet regularly in person. You can look for specific communities for your industry or for your type of business.

It's incredibly valuable to surround yourself with people who have "been there, done that," who are going through similar things to you, and who can relate to your experience and just be there for you when you need them. So, what communities are you part of, online or offline?

Disconnecting

Who's going to help you disconnect? Now, in the section on Belief above, I indicated the importance of distancing yourself, to some extent, from your immediate circle when you first start your journey out of the 9 to 5. Your immediate friends and family will most likely project their own fears and insecurities onto you, and you'll need to incubate your ideas to protect them from criticism, at least in the early stages.

You'll need to choose selectively who you want to share what information with, and it's likely that you'll be able to be more open with people who perhaps don't know you and your 'past self' so well. However, you do also need people who *don't* get the whole entrepreneurship thing, who aren't obsessed with marketing funnels and email sequences and webinar software and conversions and, and, and… That's where your friends come back into the picture.

When I was working at Procter and Gamble, in my corporate days, I had a group of existing friends who were outside of the company bubble. When we met after work, they would kindly ask, "Hey, how was your day?" I'd say, "Argh, it was so stressful," they'd say, "oh, poor you," and then we'd move on to talk about something else. On the other hand, some of my colleagues had an immediate friendship circle that included only other work colleagues and, at least this was my impression, they would always be on their Blackberries together, talking about work and the latest launch.

Sometimes you need to disconnect – even when you're doing work that you're passionate about and building a purpose-driven business. You don't want to be talking about those funnels and lead magnets and whatever else with everybody all the time. Friends are important for that.

Expertise

A final form of support that you will need is expert guidance. Again, you've chosen to read this book, and I'm providing a certain level of support in the form of frameworks and general advice. I also offer coaching and mentoring, whether on a one-to-one basis or in the Business Incubator and Accelerator programmes (you can find out more about these at onestepoutside.com). Specifically, I'm helping you define what 'success' looks like for you, choose the right business model that will support that vision, and anchor your vision and strategies in the day-to-day schedule and actions that you're taking. I'm helping you design and build that life outside of the 9 to 5.

You might also need an expert in a specific area. For example, maybe you want to get better at sales, showing up confidently on video, or setting up an email funnel. Perhaps you want to work with someone who is an expert on money mindset, or pricing your products and services, if that's an area that you particularly struggle with. There are elements of these aspects in what I cover, but to go deeper, you will want to consult a true expert in that niche. So which experts do you have, and do you need, to guide you?

Exercise 2-4:

1. Consider the five types of support and, for each one, assess: (i) what support do you have already have, and (ii) what do you still need to put in place?
    a. Accountability
    b. Belief
    c. Community
    d. Disconnecting
    e. Expertise

Pillar 3:
Choosing the right business model

PILLAR 3:
CHOOSING THE RIGHT BUSINESS MODEL

Here we are, Pillar 3, where we're looking at choosing the right business model. Now, if you've jumped to this chapter and skipped over the first two pillars thinking, "yeah, yeah, I know all that stuff, I just want to get into the meaty bit," then I say to you, DON'T DO IT! I ask you to trust me, and the process, and go back to the beginning. Read through Pillars 1 and 2 first, because they really are going to lay the foundation for everything that we'll be looking at here in Pillar 3, and beyond.

I imagine that you're eager to get to the practical strategies – especially if you're already in business and you want to see results right away, or if you're at the beginning and you're impatient to get your business up and running. However, you first need to do the work to truly understand what it is that you want to get out of your business and life (Pillar 1) so that you can choose how you're going to get there; and you need to make sure that you have the right mindset and the confidence and resilience so that you don't self-sabotage along the way (Pillar 2).

With that in mind, I'm going to assume that you've now worked through those pieces and you're here to choose the right business model based on the vision that you've come up with. If you're just starting out, you have a unique opportunity to design your business in the right way from the very beginning. If you're already in business, you can consider how you might want to pivot your model or develop different products and services to better meet your objectives.

If you don't do this work and get clear on the right business model for you, the risk is that you'll end up copying other 'gurus' and experts as you try to implement their blueprint for success. The problem is that they may have a completely different set of life goals and financial objectives; they will certainly have a different set of skills and interests; and their definition of success is very likely different to yours.

Alternatively, you may create an 'accidental' business model where you haven't been intentional in making choices that will serve you in the long run. The likely consequence is that you'll end up working with the 'wrong' clients in a way that doesn't fit with your desired lifestyle, as you replicate the patterns from your corporate role to the point that your business is no more enjoyable or fulfilling than your full-time job.

Choosing the right business model will ultimately determine whether you'll experience that freedom, flexibility, and fulfilment that you're after. The 'right' business model is a model that fits your personal preferences, your lifestyle aspirations, and your income criteria, and that's what we're going to be looking at here.

At a high level, the kind of business that we're talking about, and that I tend to favour, is a service-based business where you are an expert in your subject matter. It's easier to hit the ground running with this kind of business without the investment in tools, inventory, storage, and so on that a product business would require. In my experience, it's also easier to make a service business work around your lifestyle.

We're talking about freelancing – where you're selling your services to other businesses or individuals; coaching or consulting – where you're providing guidance or support in your field or speciality; or teaching what you know – packaging up your expertise into workshops, courses, and programmes. In each of these models, you can leverage your existing skills, experience, and network. You might also consider a portfolio career where you're doing some combination of these.

First, we'll be getting clear on your criteria. Before you even consider any specific business models, you need to know what your criteria are, so that you can assess the different options available to you according to those criteria.

Then we'll look at identifying the ideal clients that you want to work with. We'll be looking at both companies, what we call 'B2B' or Business to Business, and individuals, what we call 'B2C' or Business to Consumer.

Next, we'll be looking at developing the products and services that are going to bring all this to life, so that you have something to offer those ideal clients that will bring in a revenue that meets your income goals.

Finally, we'll look at designing your bigger ecosystem – and what that means will become clear when we get to it.

So, let's get into Pillar 3, choosing the right business model.

GETTING CLEAR ON YOUR CRITERIA

The 'right' business model is the one that's going to get you to your vision of success; and the first step here is to get clear on your criteria that match that vision.

I'm not going to recommend a specific model as such, and we're not going to get straight into business planning now. Before we do that, I want you to look back over your notes from Pillar 1 where we explored your definition of success and started creating your vision for your life and business. We're now going to translate that vision into criteria.

If you have one specific idea that you're already working on, or you've been in business for a while and you're rethinking where you want to take it, you will be able to use these criteria to shift your business model in a better direction for you, or to guide you in evaluating new projects. If you're right at the beginning of the process, you'll be able to use your criteria to assess the different ideas that you have, and to understand which ones are worth pursuing. Some of your ideas, even if successful, won't bring you meaningful success.

What is a business model?

First, though, what is a business model? A quick Google (Expert Program Management, 2018) brings up the following definition:

> *a plan for the successful operation of a business, identifying sources of revenue, an intended customer base, your products, your details of financing*

We're going to look at these different elements. However, I want to draw your attention to the very first part, which is "a plan for the successful operation of a business".

As you know by now, success for me is not measured solely by revenue and profit – it's not just about the money. If you take nothing else away from this book, then let this be the key insight that you remember: success in your business is whatever you define as success for you. This means that the business model must support your vision, your version, of success and the lifestyle that you want. This will include the income that you want but also the number of days and hours that you want to work, the kind of work that you'll be doing, how it connects with your purpose, and so on.

If a 'coach' or salesperson on social media says to you, "Follow my strategy X to build an eight-figure business," or "I can help you become a six-figure speaker" or "best-selling author" or "[fill in the impressive result here]"… Well, maybe they can. If they're genuine, they will have achieved this result for themselves and for their clients as well. What is important, however, before you rush into implementing their strategy (and pay them big bucks to learn how to do so), is that you ask yourself what *you* are trying to achieve.

The fact that someone else has had great success with, for example, group coaching programmes that are run on a cohort basis and sold via webinars every three months – well, that doesn't mean that this is something that you want to do. Yes, maybe they can teach you how to do that; but maybe you prefer working with individuals rather than groups, or you would rather have ongoing enrolment into your programmes, or you find webinars stressful or at odds with how you want to show up in your marketing.

So, the first question is, what is your version of success? Which strategic choices do you want to make to get you there? What kind of business do you want to be running, and how does it need to support your lifestyle? We're coming back to those questions from Pillar 1: What if it all works out? More specifically, what do you want to do, be, and have? How does your ideal day unfold?

Do you want to be super visible in your marketing, publishing lots of video content, or do you prefer spreading the word by having more personal conversations? Do you want to be commuting to an office or working from home? Do you want to be out and about with other people, or do you want to be working by yourself at your computer? And yes, this is still an important piece of the puzzle, what income are you targeting? Do you want to grow as big as you possibly can, to be super rich and have an uber-luxurious lifestyle? (No judgement!) Or do you rather want to hit an income that allows you to live your life pretty much as you do now, with a little less work and a little more freedom, and that's 'enough'?

Do you want to have a big team where you're outsourcing all the work and you're the CEO focusing on business development and people management? Or are you passionate about the work that you do, and you want to keep things small, so it's only ever going to be you as a solopreneur, maybe with some associates or freelancers supporting you?

There are a few different aspects to consider in coming up with the criteria that will guide your strategic choices:

- **your practical parameters;**
- **your personal preferences; and**
- **your purpose.**

Let's look at each of these in turn.

Your practical parameters

The first aspect to consider is the practical side of things, your practical criteria. What is your minimum take-home salary, and what is your ideal or 'stretch' target? Maybe you have an, "I can get by with this" amount in mind, and then also an, "I would like to move towards that" amount.

What are the hours that you want to be working? Do you want to continue working Monday to Friday but perhaps shorten the day, starting later or finishing earlier? Do you want to only work three days a week? What does your ideal day, week, and year look like?

How flexible do you need to be, in terms of when you're working, and where you're working? Do you have a maximum commute that you'd tolerate, if you were going to commute to clients' offices? Do you not want to go to clients' offices at all? How much do you want to travel? Do you want to be jet setting around the world? Do you want to be travelling nationally, locally, or not at all?

How do you want your business to fit around your kids and any childcare responsibilities? How does it need to fit around whatever your partner does in their work? How does the business need to provide for you and your family, so that you can continue to comfortably pay the bills and maintain your lifestyle? Do you have a chronic health condition that you need to consider when designing your business? These are some of the questions to think about when it comes to the practical parameters as to what your business and work can and can't look like.

Your practical parameters – setting a target income

Before moving onto the second aspect, your personal preferences, I want to 'double click' on the income and salary piece here.

As part of your criteria, you will of course need to be earning a certain amount of money. That is, unless you're in the very fortunate position where you have a partner who can financially support you and your family, or you're sitting on a massive inheritance… But I'm assuming here that you want to earn a certain independent income with your business. In my experience, there are three main strategies for setting your target:

- **matching your corporate salary;**
- **calculating a bottom-up figure; or**
- **setting a top-down figure.**

The first strategy is matching your current or previous corporate salary. This is a quick way of setting yourself a target in your business. However, let's say that you want to match a net salary of £100,000; well, this means you'll need to earn quite a bit more than that in gross revenue in your business. Remember that you'll have business expenses, you're paying taxes as well (income tax as a sole trader; as a limited company, you'll also pay corporation tax and VAT). Not to mention the fact that you'll no longer have employee benefits such as a pension, health insurance, gym memberships, and so on. If you want to match your current salary of £100,000, you might need to be generating £150,000 or even £200,000 in gross sales, so make sure you're taking that into account. With that in mind, taking your current salary provides a first easy benchmark for your business.

The second strategy is to calculate a 'bottom-up' figure. This means looking at your living expenses (including rent or mortgage, groceries, and other necessities but also things like travel, a personal trainer, a cleaner…) and your business expenses (again, including necessities like web hosting and accounting but also considering marketing, admin support, and professional development including coaching and training). This will give you a minimum figure to hit to cover your business expenses and sustain your lifestyle.

The third and final strategy is to choose a dream, 'top-down' number. Whether it's an easy round number of six or seven figures, or half a million, or whatever makes sense in your currency, you're choosing a dream number that would give you true financial freedom. It may seem like a far-off fantasy or, as you develop your business model and do the maths, you may find it's not as fantastical as you might think.

So, those are three ways in which you can arrive at your target revenue. For now, don't overthink it. You can calculate all three numbers if you'd like, so that you have different ranges to aim for.

Once you have a target revenue, it's helpful to translate this into a ballpark hourly rate. You can do this by, first, calculating your 'billable' hours in a year. If you were working 9 to 5, 5 days a week, 52 weeks of the year, this would give you 2,080 hours in a year. But that's not what we are aiming for here! How many weeks per year do you want to be working? How many days per week? How many hours per day?

Don't forget that not every working hour will be 'billable'. You'll also be doing admin, accounting, business development, and so on. Plus, you simply won't have the capacity to fill every minute of the day with 'active working' such as delivering workshops, coaching, and back-to-back calls. Your billable hours could end up being anything from 20% to 80% of your total, depending on your chosen business model.

Once you have your billable hours in a year, you can calculate your ballpark hourly rate by dividing your overall annual target revenue by the number of billable hours.

Billable hours/year = % billable hours x hours/day x days/week x weeks/year

Ballpark hourly rate = annual target income / billable hours/year

For example, let's say that I have a target revenue of £100,000, and I want to work 9 months of the year, 3 days a week, for 6 hours a day, and that I estimate that 40% of my working hours will be billable.

Billable hours/year = 40% billable hours x 6 hours/day x 3 days/week x 40 weeks/year = 288 hours

Ballpark hourly rate = £100,000 / 288 = £347.22

Note that I'm not saying that you now would need to charge £347.22 per hour. However, this figure will give you an indication of what you need to be earning to hit your overall financial targets.

So, that's the first part of coming up with your criteria, considering your practical parameters.

Your personal preferences

The second cluster of criteria are your personal preferences. These preferences reflect the way in which you like to operate.

Perhaps you're a very social person and you love working in a team. You know that you don't want to be working at home by yourself the whole time, and instead you want to be out and about, going from client to client, location to location. Or, perhaps, you love working diligently at your computer by yourself, and the complete autonomy and flexibility that comes with this.

Do you feel that you'd like to work with businesses? Is there a particular kind of business that you're drawn to? Maybe you'd like to leverage your corporate experience and continue to work with big corporations but from an external perspective, where you'd be helping to solve the problem that you experienced while on the inside? Or would you rather have a change and work with small businesses, start-ups, or charitable organisations? Do you feel a pull towards working with individuals instead?

This is the distinction of B2B, Business to Business, or B2C, Business to Consumer. We'll look at these two different strategies in the next step but, for now, do you have any preferences? Are you thinking, "Oh, my goodness, no, I don't want to work with corporates anymore"? Or are you more than happy to keep nurturing those existing relationships?

Do you prefer going deep with a small number of individuals or organisations? Perhaps you'd like to come into a company for a six-month project, or work with individual clients for a 12-month engagement, providing an end-to-end solution where you're helping them achieve a significant transformation? Or do you want to impact as many people as possible, and you don't mind this being at a lower level as a result?

For example, I have my Business Academy, a self-paced course where in theory at least I can have hundreds of participants because there is limited live interaction with me. However, this means that there won't be as much of a transformation and therefore I will be charging less for the course than if you were to work with me in my Business Incubator or Accelerator programme, or in a one-to-one capacity. (You can find out more about these programmes at onestepoutside.com.) I've reached the point in my business where I offer these different possibilities, and you can absolutely work towards this as well, if you find that you enjoy a mix.

So, do you prefer to work with a handful of clients, going deep and helping them achieve a massive transformation? Or do you prefer large groups where you're reaching as many people as possible? These are all your personal preferences.

Your purpose

The final piece of the puzzle involves looking again at your purpose. What are the different elements that you want to make sure that you bring into your business?

What are the skills you want to be using? Maybe you want to continue to leverage skills that you have been using in your corporate job, or there might be others that you've been neglecting? Perhaps there's an element of creativity or some other talent that you haven't been allowed to express? What do you want to continue to use, and what do you want to add into the mix?

What kind of work do you want to be doing? What do you absolutely love? Do you enjoy analysing the data, or coming up with innovative solutions? Do you thrive when you're teaching, or enabling your team to achieve their goals? What is the nature of the kind of work that you love doing?

What are the causes you want to be involved in? What's the impact you want to make? What do you care about? Is there a personal journey that's important to you, or are there particular people you want to be working with? What's your bigger mission?

I won't go into the fourth circle of your purpose, the monetisation piece, here, as we've already talked about setting your revenue target.

Choosing your 'non-negotiables'

Those are the three aspects of your criteria to consider: your practical parameters; your personal preferences; and your purpose.

You might end up with a long 'shopping list' of criteria that feels impossible to fulfil. To narrow down your list, try to clarify what's a 'nice to have'; what's important (but not strictly speaking necessary); and, above all, what is non-negotiable. Your non-negotiables might include, "I must earn at least x for this to be a viable business," "I absolutely cannot work on weekends," and so on.

Remember that the definition of a business model is "a plan for the successful operation of your business" – and you get to define what that 'success' is for you.

Exercise 3-1:

1. What are your criteria for making this work for you? Consider:
   a. the practical parameters;
   b. your personal preferences; and
   c. your purpose.

   Once you have your different criteria, underline the ones that are non-negotiable. While you may need to compromise on some of the more 'nice-to-haves', at least in the short term, you want to be crystal clear on your non-negotiables.

2. Have a go at calculating a ballpark hourly rate based on your overall target income and using your criteria for how many hours, days, and weeks you want to work.

Billable hours/year = % billable hours x hours/day x days/week x weeks/year

Ballpark hourly rate = annual target income / billable hours/year

This ballpark rate will give you an indication of the kind of value that you need to be providing, the calibre of clients you need to be working with, and the kind of products and services you need to be creating and delivering.

IDENTIFYING YOUR CLIENT TARGET

Having clarified your criteria, we can now move on to looking at the business model itself. We'll start with identifying your client target.

In my marketing days at Procter & Gamble, we used the Who-What-How framework. We started with the Who, that is, the consumer; then we developed the brand, the product – the What; and, finally, we developed the marketing campaign, the How. Our CEO at the time always used to say, "consumer is boss" (Lafley, 2008). We would focus on developing insights about that consumer or customer and then we would develop better products and campaigns based on those insights.

Now, in the type of business we're talking about here, the whole point is that you're designing a business that you're going to love. It's not just a case of seeing a problem in the market and then jumping onto it and solving it. The product-market fit also needs to be a fit with you, so that's an important caveat. Nevertheless, I still agree with starting with an understanding of who you want to be working with and what their problems are. You can't just say, "Hey, I really want to do this," put something out into the world, and disregard whether there's a need for what you're creating.

In marketing, you may hear the advice that you should "give them what they want" – because that's what they're asking for, that's what they're willing to pay for – but then you, as the expert, should also "give them what they need".

So, for example, people will come to me wanting more clients, more money, and perhaps to learn some specific marketing tactic. That's fine, and I can and will cover that. However, I will also bring them back to the foundations. I'll help them get clear on their definition of success, the vision for their life and business; shift their mindset and develop more confidence and resilience; choose the right business model that will get them to their vision; build a personal brand that lives above and beyond any specific tactic or even business; and design their work-life integration so that it works for them. I know that this – which you'll recognise as the 5 Pillars in this book – is what they truly need to be successful.

We've started by looking at your vision, your criteria, and understanding what it is that you want to do; this is the internal side of things, and it's absolutely fundamental. Now, though, we need to look to the external world. What kind of people do you want to be working with? What are the problems that they're struggling with? How would they articulate those challenges? What is it that they want?

There are certain universal needs and desires that drive people's buying behaviour. We all want to make some kind of gain (more time, more money) and avoid any loss; we want to avoid pain and experience more pleasure; we want to increase our own personal comfort and boost our social status. In order to create something that people truly want, you will need to speak to one or more of these desires.

As much as you want to speak to a universal desire, however, you also need to be specific. Seth Godin (2013), a bit of a guru in the marketing world, has said that "If you are trying to reach everyone, I'll know you're likely to reach no one." And this is important. Sometimes, when I ask clients, "Who do you want to work with? Who can you help?" They'll say, "Oh, I want to work with everybody; I can help everybody." That's a lovely sentiment – but not so effective when it comes to your marketing strategy.

Why you need to get more specific

Having a more specific target will help you design better products and services, because you can design them with this specific target in mind. You can address their problems, speak to their pain points, and help them create the results that they are after.

It will also allow you to be more specific in your messaging. If you have a real ideal client in mind – often, it might be a past version of you – then you can speak in a compelling way to that person. Your website, your social media content… this can all be designed to speak to one specific client, one problem, and one solution.

Now, if you're like most people, the idea of being so specific – the much talked about act of 'niching' – will feel uncomfortable. The fear is that you'll be putting other people off, and, especially at the start of your business, shouldn't you be grateful for any client who comes along? The truth, though counterintuitive, is that you'll attract more people with a specific message for a specific audience. Not only will that specific target resonate more strongly with your message, but you'll also get others coming to you saying, "I saw that you work with this type of person (or business), but could you also help me?" And at that point, if the client is a fit, you can still choose to say "yes".

Being specific as to who you're speaking to and what you're saying also allows you to be more targeted in your marketing and, therefore, more cost effective. If you know that you're working with retirees who aren't too savvy with the internet, you're probably not going to need to spend time and money on TikTok. If you're working with a younger audience, that might be a great place to focus. You need to know where your target is active and, to do that, you need to know who that target is.

Knowing and understanding what your target wants and needs will also make you more credible as an expert and a specialist. Now, I see myself as a generalist rather than a specialist, and I'm sure that many of you, like me, aspire to the idea of a portfolio career where you get to pursue your different passions and keep things interesting with different projects. The most effective profile, I believe, is to be a 'T-shaped generalist'. This means that you can absolutely have a broad set of skills and experience (that's the horizontal bar at the top of the T); but then you also want to go deeper in a specific area (that's the vertical bar of the T). This balance allows you to understand the broader context while also offering specific expertise.

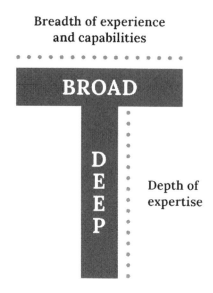

Figure 12: The specialising generalist or 'T-shaped' professional

I'll be the first to admit that my own message of "escaping the 9 to 5", "building a business and a life outside of the 9 to 5", and "reimagining success" is rather broad. But I am speaking to a specific client target: an experienced corporate professional who has seen traditional success in their career; a specific problem: they want to quit their jobs, but they lack the confidence and knowledge as to how to do so without sacrificing their income and therefore their lifestyle; and a specific result: I'll help them translate their skills and expertise into a profitable, and enjoyable, business.

Finally, having a specific target allows people to recommend you to others in their network. If I know exactly what you do and who you work with, I will immediately recognise someone that you can help, and tell them, "You must speak to so-and-so, they are the go-to expert on this topic." If you're unclear about what you do and who you help, you make such referrals very difficult.

Now that I've made a case for why you need to choose a specific client target, let's move on to helping you do just that. We're going to look at two options, broadly speaking:

- **B2B, Business to Business; and**
- **B2C, Business to Consumer.**

An effective business model may ultimately involve a combination of the two and I will be asking you to explore both options. However, you'll want to start with one or the other so that you can focus your efforts in the short term.

B2B, Business to Business

First, then, what are the advantages and disadvantages of Business to Business?

Well, businesses will generally have greater purchasing power. Bigger budgets mean bigger projects, which in turn means fewer projects. You can focus on a small number of lucrative projects with a handful of clients, instead of having to hustle to get lots of low-level projects from a long list of different clients. Coming from that corporate background yourself, you'll also have a good understanding of their challenges, their ways of working, and the language that they use; and, on the other side, they're going to value your skills and experience. Finally, larger companies will have multiple teams and departments, which means that, once you're 'in', you can sell and deliver the same solution to other departments.

When I first quit my job at Procter & Gamble, I landed on my feet with my consulting business and was earning as much as, or more than, my previous salary thanks to two or three clients and projects per year. The P&G name on my CV was instantly recognisable and respected, and that put me in a strong position from the start. It also meant that I had a network of other ex-P&Gers who would recommend me to their new employers. And, coming back to that idea of being a specialist, my digital marketing skills were in high demand.

However, there are also disadvantages with the B2B model, as I see it. Precisely because of all those teams and departments, there is greater complexity with many different stakeholders. You may have productive conversations with HR, for example, but they may not be the budget owners or the ultimate decision makers. Decisions will take longer, which means you'll have a longer sales cycle, and it can take months and months of emails and calls from the first point of contact through to securing the contract. You may also need more formal qualifications with those larger companies. Executive coaching, for example, tends to require an official accreditation by an organisation like the ICF, the International Coaching Federation. A final disadvantage – just a detail, but an annoying one – is the convoluted process of getting set up as an official vendor, challenging their standard payment terms, chasing late payments, and so on.

If you do want to work Business to Business – in any case, I'd encourage you to consider it – then you'll want to go back and look at your criteria. Are there specific industries where you have experience, or a particular interest? What about the location? Do you want to focus on local businesses because you want to be there in person, and you don't want a long commute or lots of travel? Or do you want to go international and either travel extensively or offer solely virtual services? What size company and what type of company? Private corporations, start-ups, charities…?

Once you have the criteria for your B2B target, you can go deeper on the types of problems that these companies are facing. What do they want, and need? Private companies ultimately want to increase sales, cut costs, increase profit, and so on; but what else? They need to implement wellness initiatives, and may have Diversity, Equity, and Inclusion (DEI) or Environmental, Social and Governance (ESG) requirements.

I'd suggest that you come up with a list of 15-20 companies as your 'wish list' of companies you'd like to work with. You can then research, understand, and target these companies in your marketing and sales.

It's a bit like if you were to apply to a job at one of these companies. Most people's go-to approach is to upload a generic CV to the online portals of hundreds of companies and then wonder why they're not getting any offers. It's much more powerful to have a small number of companies that you're targeting, that you've researched, where you understand their culture, goals, and challenges, and you have a real drive to want to work there. The same applies here, in your business. You want to have this shortlist of companies that fit your niche, that you really understand, and where you know that you can help them.

Once you have your list, you can set up a Google Alert so that you know what's going on, and you can follow them on LinkedIn. That means both the company, by the way, and relevant individuals who are working there. We'll get to this in the personal brand piece, in Pillar 4, but, for now, the good news is that you're not going to have to dive straight into selling mode. At this point, we're talking about connecting with key stakeholders, commenting on their posts, and showing up in their feed as a credible expert in the industry.

So, those are the initial steps when focusing on the B2B approach: getting clear on your criteria, understanding their wants and needs, coming up with your client wish list, researching the companies, and connecting with key stakeholders on LinkedIn.

B2C, Business to Consumer

The second option to consider is the B2C, or Business to Consumer, approach.

In my experience, there is greater flexibility here, and a more even balance of power. Working with individuals, you're working with your peers; when you're entering a large corporation, it's more likely that you'll have to fit into existing processes and procedures, and you'll have more limited negotiating power. You will also have more personal relationships when you're working with individuals – although with B2B, of course, you are also working with individuals within the company, and you can absolutely nurture those personal relationships there as well.

I would argue that you can develop a more diversified income with B2C because you're working with more different people. If one client stops working with you or a new client starts, that's easier to manage with individuals than if you have two or three big corporate clients, where one chooses a different supplier or stops investing in your area and from one day to the next you've lost a third of your income.

An individual won't necessarily demand a certain formal qualification. Using the coaching example, most people outside of the industry aren't even familiar with the official bodies that exist, while you can also build your credibility in other ways. We'll talk about this in the personal branding section.

The downside, of course, and the other side of the coin, is smaller budgets in B2C, and therefore lower spending. That, in turn, means that you'll need more clients. Individuals might also be harder to identify and harder to reach in the sense that, for example, I can't see on someone's LinkedIn profile that they want to leave their job; I can't see that they're struggling in their business, or that their work-life balance is suffering. People don't necessarily share on their feed that they have an autoimmune disease, or that they want to lose weight – and messaging someone to say, "hey, you could do with using my weight loss services!" would not be appreciated. When you're working B2B, you can more easily target a specific job title in a specific company in a specific industry.

B2C is also a more cluttered market, because there are so many individuals, and so many people working with individuals too, and there is a lot of noise out there. Individual clients can also be harder to sell to as well, although perhaps that's a limiting belief. Companies are used to being sold to; they're used to investing their budget in external experts and suppliers. An individual doesn't usually have a budget allocated to coaching, or to personal training or nutrition, and they might believe they can and should manage by themselves.

If you choose to work Business to Consumer, then there are two things to consider in understanding your target: demographics, and psychographics.

DEMOGRAPHICS	PSYCHOGRAPHICS
Age	Attitudes
Gender	Values
Marital status	Beliefs
Education	Lifestyle
Employment status	Personality
Income	Interests

Figure 13: Understanding your B2C client target

The demographics are what you would usually think of in terms of a 'client avatar'. If you were to do Facebook ads, for example, you might target 18- to 25-year-olds, female, single, with a university education, employed in the finance industry, and so on.

Beyond those basic demographics, you also need to consider psychographics. These are more nuanced, and you can't necessarily translate them directly into targeted advertising. These will instead come through in the products and services that you develop and in your messaging. What are their attitudes, beliefs, and values? What kind of lifestyle do they lead, what are their personality traits, and their interests?

You might have multiple targets, but I'd encourage you to choose one for the purpose of getting started. In my business, for example, I might consider a primary target of men and women, aged 30 to 40, with a university education, in a senior director role in a corporation (perhaps specific high-performance industries like consumer goods, finance, law), and with a high family income – those are the demographics. Then there are the psychographics: they want a better work-life balance but don't want to sacrifice their status and income, they value family along with their comfortable lifestyle, they like to travel, they have a lot of interests outside of work... And I can dig further and paint a very rich and holistic picture of that ideal client.

A note on income

As you consider B2B and B2C, do remember to look back on your revenue targets. We are going to return to this in the next chapter as we start developing products and building out the ecosystem for your business. For now, though, let's just do a bit of simple maths.

Let's say your revenue target is £100,000. Well, there are a few different ways in which you can hit that target. For example:

- 2 x big corporate clients each paying £50,000;
- 10 x mid-sized companies each paying £10,000;
- 50 x individual clients each paying £2,000;
- 100 x individual clients each paying £1,000;
- 1,000 x customers each paying £100;

...and so on.

This little exercise illustrates the palpable difference between securing two big lucrative projects with corporate clients (or individuals, for that matter, if they are high-net-worth individuals and it's a very premium service) and selling, say, a mini course to 1,000 individual clients. And can you see how it's 'easier' to get two clients, even at a much higher price, than it is to get 1,000 customers, when you're selling something more cheaply? We'll look at this in the next chapter.

A checklist

Before we move on from the ideal client, I want to walk you through a little checklist that you can use to assess what you've come up with, both for B2B and B2C.

Do they have a problem you can solve?

Are they aware of the problem?

Are they willing and able to pay?

Can you get in front of them?

Are you relatable and credible?

Do they share your core values?

Will they respect your boundaries?

Figure 14: The client checklist

First, do they have a problem that you can solve? If so, are they aware of the problem? And are they willing, and able, to pay? These first three questions are incredibly important. You're giving yourself a really hard time if you first need to educate people on the fact that "this is the problem you have," then persuade them that there is a solution, and only then start to convince them that you are the one to provide that solution.

It's much easier if they are already aware of the problem, they're actively looking for a solution, and you're swooping in to say, "hey, work with me!" Then you can focus on demonstrating that you're the most credible and effective person to help them out.

I have a colleague who has a business that solves a problem that, in fact, people aren't aware of. As a result, he needs to do a lot of education around the risks and issues that exist before he can get to offering his services as the solution. It's not impossible, but it's certainly much easier if they already know that they have a problem that you can solve.

In another scenario, one of my clients was struggling to get traction for her services. Together, we uncovered that the people she was targeting, although in need of her help, would not self-identify as such. The very people who need, let's say, leadership coaching, are the ones who probably won't know or admit that they need it. A bad manager often won't recognise that they are bad at managing. A person in need of Diversity, Equity and Inclusion training often won't raise their hand to ask for it. If you're trying to sell to somebody and you first need to persuade them, "Hey, you're really rubbish, you need this course," then that becomes very difficult.

You want your ideal client to be aware, and be willing to admit, that they have a problem. You also want them to be looking for, and willing to pay for, a solution. There are countless people I come across in my personal life and in the online space who are fed up with their jobs and want to find a way to quit to work for themselves. Most of those people, however, either don't believe that there is something to be done about it or are unwilling to consider coaching and mentoring to get the support they need to make it happen. I need to get very granular in identifying the ones who are willing, so that I can focus my energy there.

Next, from a marketing perspective, the question is: can you get in front of these clients? If you're choosing a target where you have no network and no connections, then, again, you're making your life quite difficult. Moreover, are you relatable and credible to that target? This doesn't mean that you have to be from the exact same background, although that can help. With my corporate consumer goods marketing background, I have a natural network and relatability with others who come from a similar background. That means I can more easily connect with those ideal clients, both in practical terms of finding each other and at an emotional level in my messaging.

Finally, but perhaps most importantly, does your client target share your core values, and will they respect your boundaries? These two are not questions that most business coaches will ever ask, but they are crucial considerations in the context of redefining success, designing a business that you'll love, and making work-life integration work for you.

So, in terms of the industry you're choosing to work with, but also in terms of the employees and individuals you're working with: do they share your values of, let's say, putting family first, prioritising work-life balance, or the fundamental principles of ethics and integrity? Will they respect your boundaries? Of course, this requires you to identify, communicate, and enforce your boundaries, and we'll look at this in the final section, Pillar 5, on work-life integration.

Let's say you're thinking of working with a legal firm that has a traditional working culture of working long hours, late into the night and over the weekends, and expects you to do the same. That might not be the best client for you, if you're looking to reduce your hours and create more balance and flexibility in your schedule. Spend some time thinking about whether your chosen target will share your values, and if they will respect your boundaries when you communicate them.

Exercise 3-2:

1. Consider the Business-to-Business, B2B, target:
    a. What are the criteria (industry, size, location)?
    b. What types of problems are they facing?
    c. What is your wish list of companies that you'd like to work with?
2. Consider the Business-to-Consumer, B2C, target:
    a. What are the demographics?
    b. What are the psychographics?

3. For both the B2B and B2C target that you've identified, run through the checklist to see if you're on the right track:
    a. Do they have a problem you can solve?
    b. Are they aware of the problem?
    c. Are they willing and able to pay?
    d. Can you get in front of them?
    e. Are you relatable and credible?
    f. Do they share your core values?
    g. Will they respect your boundaries?

If you're answering "no" to a few of these, you might want to go back and consider a different target.

CREATING YOUR PRODUCTS AND SERVICES

You've got your criteria for the business model that will get you to your version of success – your practical parameters, your personal preferences, and your purpose. And you've got an idea of who you want to be working with in terms of your ideal clients – B2B, Business to Business, and B2C, Business to Consumer. Now, we're going to bring these two things together, and look at how you're going to solve your chosen clients' problems.

Taking your criteria and taking your ideal client target and their problem, how can you best solve that problem? How will you deliver your solution? More concretely, this means looking at the products and services that you are going to create. You want these to be effective and convenient for your client, but also convenient and enjoyable for you.

Choosing how to deliver the solution

In choosing how you're going to solve your ideal client's problem, you need to remember your criteria, including your practical parameters, your personal preferences, and your purpose. This includes the financial aspect, to give you the income that you're looking for, and we'll get to that when we look at pricing. Let's look at some different choices and considerations when it comes to delivery.

Do you want to deliver your service on a one-to-one basis, or one-to-many? As a coach, for example, I can do individual coaching, or I can come into a corporation and do executive leadership coaching with individuals; I can speak to a larger audience via running workshops and group coaching sessions; or I can create and sell a course, which I can sell to the masses. To take another example, as a graphic designer, you can design and deliver a logo to one person, or one business, at a time; you can design and sell logo templates that lots of people can download and adapt; or you can create a course and teach groups of graphic designers how to build a successful business as a graphic designer.

Ask yourself, is it more effective to deliver your solution individually, where you can work closely with a small number of people and go deep? Or is it better, and more important to you, to reach a larger audience with your solution while accepting that you can't be as closely involved?

Do you want to deliver your work virtually or in person? Is the energy better and is it more interactive and effective to run the session live, or do you need the flexibility in your schedule to have it be virtual and even pre-recorded? Of course, there could be a combination of both.

You need to consider how effective a particular solution is as well as your own personal preferences, your lifestyle, and how the different options fit into your schedule.

There's another important distinction in terms of how you deliver the service. Are you coaching, consulting, mentoring, teaching… or are you 'doing the thing'? Are you providing a 'done-for-you' service or 'done with you'? Are you going off to work on something and then presenting the client with a finished product, or are you guiding and supporting them to get to the end result?

Then there is the length of engagement. Is it a one-off? Perhaps the initial engagement is a one-off but then, as you gain their trust, your client will want and need more ongoing support? Would you prefer to come in, do your thing, and then head off to the next project and client? Or would you want to stay there and oversee the end-to-end implementation to get real results, knowing that you would find that work more rewarding?

So those are some aspects to consider: one to one or one to many, virtual or in person, live or pre-recorded, the mode of delivery, and the length of engagement. Remember that it comes down to your criteria and preferences, as well as the client's needs and expectations.

Progression through your services

As you're thinking about how you're going to deliver your solution, you're probably coming up with quite a few different options. While you can't do all of them – at least, not right away – you do want to consider how multiple products and services might fit together. You're not just thinking about one service in isolation but looking at a menu of services that you can offer your client. This involves structuring your services so that there is a hierarchy of options for the client to choose from, depending on their needs and budget. It also involves offering them some means of progression or journey from one service to another.

There are three types of progression that I want you to consider:

- **progression in terms of pricing and value;**
- **progression in terms of the client journey; and**
- **progression in terms of the commitment.**

We'll look at each of these options now, along with examples.

Progression in terms of pricing

The first, perhaps most obvious, way in which you might provide progression is in terms of the pricing. You might offer a low-touch programme, a medium-touch, and a high-touch. What does this mean?

Well, as a 'low-touch' you might offer a self-directed course with no live element. Here, you're teaching via pre-recorded content and there's no time commitment on your side. The client gets a workbook, they get a video or audio series, and they can work through it at their own pace. There is no direct interaction with you and therefore you will be able to offer this programme at a lower price. It's arguably also the lowest value because you're not providing any tailored support, guidance, or accountability.

A medium-touch offering could be a group programme where there's an element of personal support but you're delivering it in a group setting. So, you might offer live group calls where clients get 5-10 minutes in the 'hot seat'. There might be a membership site where they can work through the content in their own time, plus a Facebook group or forum where they can interact with the community. This is a mid-range offer.

The final, high-touch, offering could include individual support from you via one-on-one calls, personalised feedback, and maybe even meeting in person. And, of course, this kind of programme will be priced at a higher level.

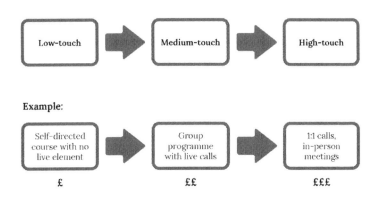

Figure 15: Progression in pricing and value

So that's one type of progression to consider, offering low touch, medium touch, and high touch, with a corresponding price increase along the way. If you've spent any time on my website or in my community, you might recognise these options in my own offering:

- the Business Academy is my low-touch offering, a self-paced course;
- the Business Incubator and Accelerator are group programme options and medium touch; and, finally,
- one-to-one coaching and mentoring is my high touch.

You can read more about these programmes to understand the nuances at onestepoutside.com.

A client could come into your ecosystem at the lower level, signing up to do a course and then continuing to invest in a group or individual programme to get more support. Or they might just go straight in at the level that they feel provides best value for them. They might prefer one to one because they're busy executives and want the most effective solution in the shortest amount of time; or they might invest in your group programme because they're lonely solopreneurs and looking for the community aspect. You are offering these different options, and you can propose, and the client can choose, the best one for their budget and preferences.

Progression in terms of the client journey

Another type of progression you could provide relates to the client's journey. This one is very powerful, because you're supporting them through the different stages where they will have different needs, giving them somewhere to go within your ecosystem. It's more expensive and time consuming to get a new client than it is to continue working with an existing client who is already bought into your offering.

This is not about manipulating people into buying more than they need but rather continuing to support them. If I've run a one-off workshop on work-life balance, let's say, for a B2B client, then that's great but it's unlikely to completely change the game for their employees. It would have more of an impact if I came back for a series of workshops, or if I could provide ongoing coaching and implementation support for the individuals in the team. If I've supported a B2C client in arriving at a decision that, yes, they do want to quit their job and start a business, then the obvious next step for me is to help them design that business.

Not every company, or individual, will choose to continue to invest with you; but there is the option available. There is a possibility of progressing to a more advanced level, to a deeper level, or to a degree of ongoing accountability.

Your first offering might take the client from point A to point B; your second from B to C; and your third from C to D. You might even have a 'flagship offering' that takes them straight from A to D. What you probably don't want to do is try to take them from A all the way to Z. In my case, I'm not going to create an offering where I promise to take you from "I don't know what I want to do" through to "I'm making eight figures and living my best life in Bali."

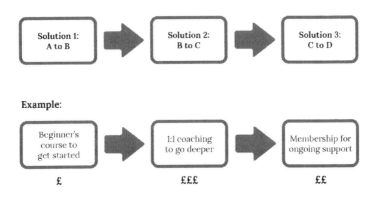

Figure 16: Progression in the client's journey

Perhaps you start by offering a course for beginners. Once they've completed the course, and learned the basics, they might want to upgrade to a coaching programme where you will tailor what they've learned to their specific situation and take it to a more advanced level. Finally, they might progress into an ongoing membership with a focus on implementation and maintenance.

This could work well in fitness and nutrition, for example. An initial course teaches you the basic principles and you start to see results. You get to know the style of the expert in question, and you see that they are credible in what they offer. You choose to work with them one on one to get a programme that's tailored to your individual goals and lifestyle. Once you've achieved your health or fitness goals, you can graduate into a group membership where you get the accountability to maintain your results over a longer period.

Again, you might recognise this type of progression in my services as well – and, yes, you can absolutely have more than one type of progression across your services:

- I offer the Business Academy course as a first port of call, along with individual workshops where you can get to know me and my style.
- If you then find that you want more support to get bigger and better results, you can choose to work with me in the Business Incubator, to get from "I have an idea" to "I have a clear business model and a pipeline of clients, and I am now ready to quit my job."
- Finally, you can graduate into the Business Accelerator, which provides ongoing training, mentoring, and a community to get you sustainable results.

Again, you can read more at onestepoutside.com.

Progression in terms of commitment

The third way in which you might offer progression is in terms of the level of commitment.

Let's consider a B2B customer, a company. The middle option, let's say, your 'flagship programme' that you want to offer, is a bespoke strategy in your area of expertise. However, you're new to the industry, they've never heard of you, and they might not want to go straight in with approving the £50,000 proposal that you've sent them.

You might instead offer them an initial workshop to introduce them to your approach – on work-life balance, innovation, diversity, or whatever your subject matter happens to be. If they buy into your approach, and the feedback on the session is overwhelming positive, then you might propose that you come in and create that more comprehensive strategy for them. Finally, you might offer to stay around for a bit longer to oversee the implementation of the strategy.

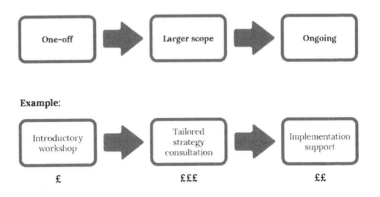

Figure 17: Progression in the level of commitment

You can see that the level of commitment increases as you progress. A new client might not be ready for all the amazing things that you could do for them, but they would be willing to give you a test run with a one-off workshop or talk. Then, when you over-deliver on expectations and dazzle them with your solution, you can upsell them to the next level of commitment.

Pricing your services

Now, coming back to your revenue goals, of course, the combination of all the different products and services that you come up with is going to add up to your total revenue. So again, if you take a target revenue of £100,000, you'll need to play around with the pricing of your different products to give you the result that you're after. To get to that pricing, you need to estimate the number of clients you expect to be able to sell and deliver to.

If you've got a course – my Business Academy, for example – then it's in your interest to sell as many as possible as its delivery isn't tied to your time. Given that it will be set at a lower price point, you'll also need to sell more courses to generate a substantial income.

If you've got a group programme, consider how many people you can work with at a time. I have the Incubator and the Accelerator, and although they are designed for groups of people, I want to keep the numbers low so that I can give everyone the right level of attention.

Finally, one-to-one offers the highest price point but there are only so many hours in the day, and there is a limit to how many one-to-one projects you can deliver each month. In my case, coaching requires a lot of mental and emotional energy and so I can't just book ten client calls back-to-back. When you consider the number of clients that feels feasible for each of your programmes, alongside your total revenue target, what could that look like in terms of pricing?

We also need to consider your mindset here. Remember, and this is important, that we are talking about a financially viable business, not a hobby or a charity. While it's a wonderful sentiment to want to help people for free or for a nominal fee, we're looking for a business model that's going to replace your full-time income. That doesn't mean that you can't offer freebies or pro bono services as well; but in terms of the core business offering that's going to pay your bills, you need to be thinking strategically like a profitable business.

One way to feel better about this is to reframe selling as serving. What I mean by this is: you're not a sleazy second-hand car salesperson (an outdated image that many of us still have of selling) or a spam bot trying to push the latest scam onto an unsuspecting victim. You have identified a group with a problem, you have a solution to that problem, and you are a credible expert who can deliver that solution in an effective way. You are serving; you are helping. Or, at least, you are offering to serve, to help, to solve a problem – whether a prospect then takes you up on your offer is up to them.

So, rather than thinking of 'selling', think of serving. Focus on the value that you can provide. Focus on your expertise and your experience, the results that you can help them achieve, and the impact that you can make.

Now, the natural way to approach pricing is to look at how your competitors are pricing their services. This is fine in the sense of getting a feel for where you sit in the market, at the top end or the bottom. (And, by the way, you don't want to be at the bottom. Somewhere in the middle to top perhaps.)

However, who is to say that these other people know what they're doing in setting their prices? More to the point, you have no idea if they're even successful with that pricing, how many clients they have, and how much they're earning. You don't know what their business expenses are, their cost of living, or their lifestyle aspirations. Maybe their business model, and pricing, is working for them, and maybe it isn't. Whether it's working or not, this has limited bearing on whether it's going to work for you. Try not to get too caught up in what other people are charging.

Most importantly, as in all these things, there is no right answer. At the end of the day, it's just a number. You'll probably start with lower pricing and, as your confidence builds, you'll gradually raise your prices to correspond better with the value that you bring, and to reflect the increase in demand as well. You could charge more, you could charge less; there are others that will be charging more, and there are others charging less; and some people will tell you you're charging too much, while others will tell you you're charging too little. There is no right answer.

Increasing the value

When it comes to pricing, as well as designing your products and services more generally, the most important question is: how can you increase the value of what you offer?

In many industries and geographies, I hear people saying, "Oh, but in my space, I can't possibly charge more than this. Everyone else is charging x and there's no way I can charge more." Okay. Let's do a theoretical exercise here: what could you do to justify charging more? How could you increase the value of what you offer so that it is worth a higher price?

I remember hearing about a coach, years ago, who liked to take people out of their comfort zone. He meant it literally and would take CEOs off on skydiving trips and rock climbing and heli-skiing and whatever else, charging $100,000 for the privilege. If you're working with high-net-worth individuals, if you're offering them an incredible experience, if you're offering a concierge service where you're at their beck and call whenever they need you... well, don't you think you can charge a high premium for that?

I had a client who was looking at offering shiatsu and alternative therapies and felt she couldn't possibly charge more than the (low) going rate that she had seen, especially as she was just starting out. Together, we went through the mental exercise of imagining what she *could* do to increase the value of what she was offering. What if you had a champagne reception in the most luxurious space? If you offered a pre-consultation before the core session, and a post-consultation follow-up? If you included a set of tailored products that would help with their ailment, or a set of personalised meditation tracks?

I'm not saying it's about the amount of stuff that you're throwing in. There is always the temptation to give more and more to try to justify a higher price point. I could write a longer book for you, add more modules to my course, or add more frequent calls to my programmes... but it might make it more overwhelming for you, and less effective in getting you results. Sometimes less is more, and a client paying more is, counter-intuitively, often expecting less.

What I am saying is that you want to look at how you can make your offering more valuable to the client. How can you deliver the results in a better way – better results, faster, more fun, more effectively? Focus less on the price as such, and more on the value. Whatever your initial price that you set, if you can deliver a better and better experience for your current clients, and for each new client, then the increase in price will follow as a natural consequence.

So, lots to think about in this chapter. Go back and re-read it to really understand the nuances of these different ways of progressing through your offering, to think deeply about the problem that you're solving, and to consider how best to deliver the solution for the sake of your clients as well as your own personal preferences and criteria.

Exercise 3-3:

1. What is the main problem that you're solving?
2. How can you best deliver your solution?
3. Consider how you might design your offering to provide one of the three types of progressions:
    a. Pricing (low touch, mid touch, high touch)
    b. Client journey (A to B, B to C, C to D)
    c. Commitment level (initial one-off commitment, deeper commitment, ongoing support)

   For each of these, have a go at allocating a price for each offering and see how it sits with you.
4. Finally, whatever the price(s) you've chosen, how could you increase the value of what you offer?

MAPPING OUT YOUR ECOSYSTEM

We've arrived at the final piece, the final step, in this business model section. Congratulations on making it this far. You may want to go back and re-read certain sections; and you may feel like you haven't got things in place just yet. I applaud you for not giving up, for ploughing through, and continuing to work through the different chapters. We're going to bring quite a few different bits together now as we look at mapping out your ecosystem.

So, what is an ecosystem? The term itself comes from the natural world, while it was also used back in my corporate days where we talked specifically about the "brand ecosystem". For me, in this context, it's the experience that you create for your clients. It encompasses the different products and services that you're offering to all your different prospects and clients. Those different offers are all providing different ways of interacting with you and your brand.

We call these points of interaction 'touch points' in marketing. A new client might come to you via a podcast episode or a speaking engagement; they might read one of your emails that they've been forwarded by a friend; or they might see a post on LinkedIn. When they first arrive in your world, in your ecosystem, they'll be introduced to your content and get started with a free download or a short video as they begin to explore what you offer. Ultimately, they'll move on to working with you and pay for one (or more) of your services.

Some people will come in, BOOM, "I love Anna, I want to work with her right away," – hey, it happens! – and they don't need lots of steps and hoops to jump through. Other people might be more of a slow burn. I've had clients who have been watching from the side lines over a period of *years* and then, finally, come out of the woodwork to say that they're ready to work with me. Both the 'fast' and the 'slow' clients are welcome, and you need to cater for both. You want to provide a 'fast-track' approach for clients who are ready to take immediate action, and then a slower nurturing process for the prospects that need more handholding.

Your vision for the business

Your ecosystem effectively represents your vision for your business. I'm not telling you to create all these elements right now, but rather to think about what your business could look like in the future. That way, you can 'start with the end in mind' and work your way backwards.

Likewise, don't get intimidated or overwhelmed by everything that someone else has already created. Bear in mind, for example, that I started my coaching business in 2015 and I've been layering things on ever since. When I first started, I had a simple website; I started blogging, as writing was my natural medium; I created a monthly newsletter; then I launched the Facebook group; and so on.

So, with that in mind, let me walk you through my own ecosystem… Perhaps you'll recognise some of these elements in your own journey, and in your interactions with the different touch points of my brand.

At the core, as a hub for my business, I have the website, onestepoutside.com. I have my different products and services available there on the site. I also have the podcast living on the website, and the blog. I have my free downloads or 'lead magnets' as you might have heard them called – at the time of writing, these include my Escaping the 9 to 5 Roadmap, the 5Ls Life Assessment, and the 5 Pillars Business Scorecard. All this content sits on the hub that is my website.

However, those things are also 'broadcast' out into the world. The podcast is on Apple Podcasts, Spotify, Google, Stitcher, and so on. The blog articles are published across the different social channels, along with regular posts and videos going out on Facebook, LinkedIn, Instagram, YouTube. I have my Facebook group (onestepoutside.com/community), which is a smaller community that offers more interaction and support.

Beyond my own channels, there are other external touch points. These include virtual and in-person speaking engagements; I've got my two books (this one included); and I have articles that are going out in online publications and print magazines.

You can see how all these pieces come together to form an interconnected system of online and offline, with different formats on different media channels, offering different products and services. Again, someone might interact with one of those touch points, book a call with me, and choose to invest right away. Or they might start by reading the blog, subscribing to the podcast, downloading a PDF resource, joining a live webinar... and only after all those interactions will they decide to invest (if ever).

What is the vision for your business? Things that might seem far off and impossible now aren't impossible if you extend your timeline to think three years, five years, ten years from now. If you want to be a well-known public speaker, that's totally feasible, so by all means put that on there. You might not be able to charge £20,000 for a keynote today, but it could be something to aim for in the future. If you want to be a bestselling author, then put that on there. Want to launch a podcast? Offer a library of different courses? Create an in-person retreat? Put it all on there.

An upside-down funnel

We previously looked at offering progression in terms of pricing, the client journey, and the level of commitment; now we can add to that picture with these other bits and pieces to create a more complete ecosystem. You might see this depicted as a funnel, through which people get to 'know, like, and trust' you. Prospects come in at the widest part at the top and it becomes narrower as fewer and fewer people trickle down into your business. We're going to take this funnel but think about it the other way around, like a pyramid with the peak at the top.

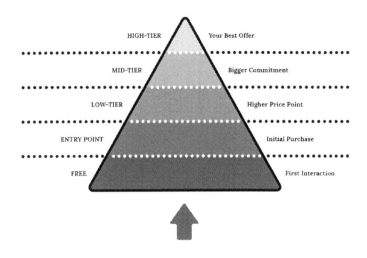

Figure 18: Building out the customer journey

In this version, you've got clients coming in from the bottom. They'll start with a first initial interaction – perhaps they'll read a post on social media, they'll click through to your profile, and they'll follow you on Instagram, connect with you on LinkedIn, or subscribe to your YouTube channel. This represents a small commitment, a tiny step, that doesn't cost any money.

Next, there is an initial purchase. It's a no-brainer price, affordable to all, but at this point they have taken their credit card out to pay you.

After that, there's another purchase, which is at a higher price point. It's still low touch, but they have invested a more substantial sum.

Then there is a bigger commitment at the next level, at a higher price point.

Finally, right at the top, they get to the 'big shebang'. They've reached the very peak of your services and they're getting the most amazing experience and achieving the best results.

This is the traditional way in which the marketing funnel is taught (albeit upside down), where you start with the 'point-of-market entry', and then gradually move to a bigger commitment in terms of both time and money. However, clients won't necessarily come in at the lowest price point and work their way up in such a linear fashion. More importantly, it makes more sense strategically for you to start at the top with your flagship offering and work your way down.

I recommend starting with your very best offer, the way in which you know that you can deliver the best solution, the most comprehensive and transformative experience for your client, in a way that you will enjoy, that they'll enjoy, and that will get you to your vision of success.

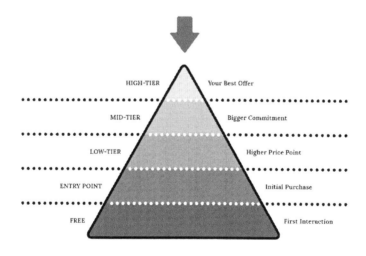

Figure 19: Starting from the top

Maybe your best offer is to work with your client for a year, end to end, start to finish, getting involved in every aspect of the project, and being there every step of the way – that will then, of course, become your highest tier offer. Now, maybe nobody will want to invest at that high level at the beginning (and maybe no one will want to invest in that solution ever). Knowing that this is your flagship offer, however, that it's what you want to be known for and that is, in your experience and given your expertise, the absolute best way that you can help somebody... you can have that in mind as you design the rest of your ecosystem.

You can always 'down-sell' people. I can recommend my full flagship solution to you, taking you from A to Z, that will cost you £10,000. You might find that's far too high an investment in terms of both time and money. Then I can propose alternative programmes that will offer a more limited result at a lower price point. You can choose to get started with the more limited offer or, sometimes, when you see the two side by side, you can decide that you do want to invest in the full programme.

You can always have these kinds of conversations, but it's much easier to drop down from a higher-level to a lower-level programme and price than it is to come in low and then try to pitch a leap up to your high-end programme.

Some clients may well come in at the bottom and work their way up, while others might buy the entry-point offering and then never do anything else. Some might come in at the mid-tier and stay there over several years. A select few will go straight for your top offering as they'll see its tremendous value. Many more, of course, will only ever consume the free content.

The One Step Outside™ funnel

To make all this conceptual talk more tangible, I'll illustrate it with my own funnel…

New people might come into my ecosystem after hearing me speak on someone else's podcast, for example. They'll come over and subscribe to my podcast, where they'll be prompted to download one of my free resources, and then they'll receive a little email sequence that tells them about me and how I can support them further. They might also join the Facebook group and be part of the free community there.

An entry point offer in my world is a book that costs less than £10. This is a great way to get a feel for who I am, to be introduced to the concepts and frameworks that I teach, and to start making changes and seeing some initial results. More recently, I've also started running one-off workshops, which I offer at a very affordable price point. Some people will come in and just buy the book, or they'll only join the workshops now and then, and they'll never do anything else – and that's fine. Others will experience this taster, recognise the value I bring, and look for opportunities to work with me more closely. (Which path will you choose, I wonder…?)

My 'low-tier' offering is the Business Academy course. I hate to call it low tier because it's incredibly comprehensive. Compared to one-to-one coaching or a live group programme, however, it's true that you are working through the 5 Pillars framework in a self-directed way with no tailored support from me.

In the mid-tier range, you can invest in the Business Incubator, which is a hybrid course, coaching, and mentoring programme that will help you design and build a business that allows you to escape the 9 to 5; or, if you already have a business, and you've worked through the Academy (or this book), you can join the Business Accelerator as an ongoing mastermind.

Right at the top, at the pinnacle of my world, you'll find one-to-one coaching and mentoring. Here you have an opportunity to go deep with me on your definition of success, to get super clear on your personal brand, or really work on your work-life integration. With one-to-one coaching, you get my undivided attention and tailored support.

So, that's what it looks like for me right now (and you can read more about all these programmes at onestepoutside.com).

Creating a roadmap

Now, remember, the intention here is not to send you off with an overly ambitious plan to try to do all these things at once. You want to start with one client problem that you're solving, one flagship product or service, and one customer journey. This way, you can focus on solving that one issue for your most ideal client, communicating that solution single-mindedly, and pushing that one product or service – at least, let's say, for the next 90 days, if not for the next year.

For example, I can choose to focus on the corporate professional who wants to escape the 9 to 5; they have started a business but aren't hitting their revenue goals or experiencing the lifestyle that they wanted. I can speak to that specific situation in my social media posts and in my emails. I can guide that professional through clear steps to take in terms of downloading my free 5 Pillars scorecard (onestepoutside.com/scorecard), booking a call, and then either joining my Business Academy as a self-study option, or getting my tailored support to help them build the business that will allow them to replace their corporate salary.

Start with one ideal client and one problem that they're facing. With that in mind, you can then design a PDF, a video, an email sequence, a free workshop, or a paid workshop – you choose the format – to solve their immediate problem. Then that will feed into your paid programme as a next step.

Alternatively, you can work backwards. With your flagship product or service in mind, you can ask yourself, what are the steps that they need to take before they're ready to work with you? What do they need to know about you? What do they need to know about the solution that you're providing? What answers do you need to provide? What results can they get, and do they need to have achieved, before they can work with you?

Starting with one-to-one

When it comes to your roadmap, there is one piece of advice that I would give you, and that is to start with one-to-one.

Whether you are a coach or consultant, a graphic designer, a shiatsu practitioner – whatever it is that you offer – I recommend that you start with delivering your solution on an individual basis.

When you're first starting out, you won't have a large audience. You can have a thriving business with even just a small audience when you're working on an individual basis, whether B2B or B2C. (In fact, even now, I don't have a huge audience.) It's so much easier, I promise, to get five individual clients – one today, one next week, one next month, and so on – investing at a higher level, than it is to get 10 or 20 or 50 to buy a cheaper service, especially all at the same time. You may think it's easier to sell at a lower price, but experience will soon confirm to you that it's easier to sell a handful of high-end services than it is to sell many low-ticket services. Starting one to one allows you to hit your revenue goals without relying on a big audience.

In the meantime, while you deliver this one-to-one service, you're going to be gaining experience and validating your solution. Before you can start teaching interior design principles to thousands of people, you need to see if your principles work for one person, one house, one room. Before I can teach my 5 Pillars framework to hundreds of clients via a pre-recorded course, I need to know that I can help even one person 'escape the 9 to 5' with my framework. And my 5 Pillars, by the way, have come from this organic process of starting with one to one, then group, and over time formalising the framework and articulating the 5 Pillars as they are today.

Starting with one on one will also allow you to develop materials as you go. As I started with individual coaching, I would develop ad hoc worksheets for my clients to support the work we were doing together. If I wanted to give them an exercise on their values, I would create a PDF that helped them do just that. I created a little book on "how to learn to say no", and another on "setting the right goals". This organic approach is much more effective and much 'safer' than spending hours on developing beautiful materials for a course or a programme before you even know if your system works, or if anyone is going to be interested.

Finally, when you start working with just a couple of people, with a handful of clients, you will be able to do an incredible job. You can over-deliver on what you promised, exceed their expectations and truly 'delight' your customer with an exceptional experience. They'll become not just happy clients but ambassadors for you and your business, giving you glowing testimonials and referring you to their friends and colleagues. Then you can go on to serve more and more clients and, when you're ready, launch a more scalable group offering.

I recommend delivering your solution first to one person, one company, before you try to be clever and create more 'passive income' too soon on your journey.

Exercise 3-4:

1. What can you provide to your prospects as a first interaction or touch point?
2. What can you offer as an initial purchase?
3. What's your low-tier offer?
4. What's your mid-tier offer?
5. What's your best, high-level, offer?
6. Finally, most importantly, what are you going to focus on over the next three months?
   a. What one client problem will you focus on in your messaging?
   b. What product or service are you going to be promoting?

Pillar 4:
Building an effective personal brand

PILLAR 4:
BUILDING AN EFFECTIVE PERSONAL BRAND

Pillar 4, where we're looking at building an effective personal brand, is one of my favourites, given my own branding and marketing background. Of course, it's very different to market yourself than it is to market a product.

Entrepreneur and author Seth Godin (2009) gives the following definition of a brand:

> *A brand is the set of expectations and memories, stories, and relationships that, taken together, account for a consumer's decision to choose one product or service over another.*

I would argue that a personal brand is the same thing when it comes to the type of business that we're building here, as a solopreneur, an expert, a freelancer, coach, consultant, designer, whatever label you feel fits. Your personal brand is how people perceive you. It's what they expect from you when they book a call, after seeing you online or reading your book, or having had various interactions with you, online or offline. It's the reason why they're choosing to work with you, and not with somebody else.

I know, it can feel a bit 'icky' to think of yourself as a brand. Here's the thing: you have a personal brand, whether you want to or not. The reality is that people will talk about you (or they won't), people will have an impression of you, whether you do something about it or not. It's simply a case of deciding if you're going to leave it up to random chance, or you're going to choose to shape it with more intentionality so that you craft a brand that serves you and the business that you're building.

People come to me because they've heard me on a podcast, they've seen me on a video, they've attended a workshop, they've read one of my books… They already see me as bringing value, and there's an element of trust and respect before they've even started working with me. From my perspective, that makes my life a whole lot easier. When they get on the phone with me, they already know that they want to work with me. At that point, they just need a final confirmation and reassurance that they're making the right decision, along with guidance on the specific programme that would be the best option for them.

An effective personal brand will elevate you beyond being just a commodity. You're no longer just an anonymous entity on a list of comparable products, a list of interchangeable service providers, where the client is just choosing in a detached manner based on price.

In the years that I've been coaching, I've had two experiences where a prospect had a long list of coaches that they were considering, and I was just one of many options. If someone is comparing me in an Excel spreadsheet where they are listing pros and cons and ticking boxes, it's highly unlikely that they'll choose me. In fact, I'd go so far as to say that it's highly unlikely that they'll choose any of the coaches on the list. Most probably, they'll feel overwhelmed, experience decision fatigue, and end up postponing the coaching to another time. I was not surprised when neither of these two prospects chose to work with me.

Your personal brand will distinguish you from your competitors because, by definition, you're one of a kind. Your specific story, your personal journey, your experience – all these things make you completely unique and incomparable to anyone else. Some would even be so bold as to say that you don't have any competitors at all because your personal brand is so specific and distinctive.

Your personal brand also helps you connect with your prospective clients because you're telling stories, demonstrating your relatability, and building trust. You can choose how vulnerable you want to be, but, in my experience, it will be your personal posts and admissions of mistakes and weaknesses that garner the most engagement in your content.

Finally, your personal brand will endure above and beyond any specific business. When I first left my corporate job, I started the Crocus Communications digital marketing consultancy; today, that business is no more. If I had poured all my marketing endeavours into Crocus Communications and hidden behind that company name, I would have had to start again from scratch when that business ended. Instead, Anna Lundberg lives on and prospers. When I decide to move on from One Step Outside™, Anna Lundberg will, again, endure.

Assuming you're now convinced that a personal brand is an indispensable and inevitable part of your business, we'll start this pillar by coming up with your headline; you might also think of this as your elevator pitch. In practical terms, it's what you're going to be using for your website home page, your social media bios, and any introductions at events and dinner parties.

Next, we'll get into developing your content strategy, the topics that you want to talk about, so that you're not just throwing up random videos and posts but rather you're crafting content that's going to support your business goals.

Part of creating your content is going to be boosting your credibility, especially if you're moving into a new space. We'll look at how you can put yourself forward as a credible expert in this new area.

Finally, we'll focus on maximising your visibility. This means amplifying the content that you're creating and giving you a platform so that new people are seeing you and entering that ecosystem that you've created for your business. If you're not getting in front of new people every week, you're not going to be able to grow your business.

So, let's get stuck into Pillar 4: building an effective personal brand.

COMING UP WITH A STRONG HEADLINE

We're going to develop an overall headline that summarises your personal brand and what you want to stand for. To help you do that, however, we'll first do some background work. And, before we even get to creating your own personal brand, I want to spend a little time on what a personal brand is, and what it isn't.

So, first: your personal brand is not built on over-sharing personal details. You don't have to (and probably shouldn't) present 100% of everything that you are and do. You don't have to post pictures of your food every day, intimate snaps of your family holiday, or videos where you talk about your latest argument with your partner. (Those things could conceivably be relevant and insightful if you are a nutritionist, if you want to demonstrate your work-life balance, or if you're a relationship coach.) Your personal brand is a curated image of who you are, and you get to choose what, and how much, you share.

Curating your personal brand, however, does not mean that you are lying or faking a perfect image. In fact, we live in a wonderful world right now where authenticity and 'realness' is valued and even celebrated. That means that you can breathe a sigh of relief as you post quick lives and short videos without worrying about perfect lighting and editing. You can present yourself in a way that you're comfortable with, rather than pretending to be someone you're not. Your personal brand is a promise to your clients and a reputation that you earn, as you show up consistently and authentically in your free content and in your paid programmes.

Finally, it's not a question of creating a brand – done – that is forever set in stone. Your personal brand is organic, a living and breathing thing. It can and will evolve with each piece of content that you post. The truth is that it will take time, and a lot of hard work; it's not something that you can create overnight.

My personal brand framework

In my marketing work at Procter and Gamble, we were using what was called a "brand equity pyramid". In the subsequent years, I've developed this personal brand framework loosely built on that pyramid.

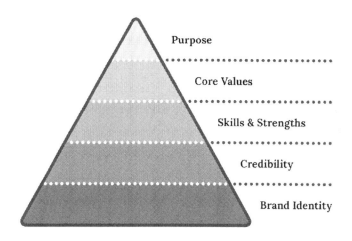

Figure 20: Your personal brand framework

At the very top of the pyramid, you'll find your purpose. We looked at your purpose in the very first section, in the first pillar, that 'ideal' middle of the Venn diagram. That's the magic sweet spot where you're doing work that you're good at and work that you love, you're making the difference that you want to make in the world, and you're earning a decent living as a result. That's the bigger purpose of your business.

At the bottom of the pyramid, you'll find what you probably more commonly associate with a brand, which is the brand identity – the logo, the pictures, and so on. When it comes to your personal brand, this is all about how you're showing up, both online and offline. This includes your logo and your imagery, as well as your elevator pitch; it's also about how you dress, how you carry yourself, and how you speak.

In the middle, you have your core values, which of course we identified in the first pillar as well; your strengths and skills, which we've also looked at; and your credibility, which we'll talk more about soon. That's the meat of your brand, as it were. For now, though, we're going to focus on the top, where you have your purpose, and the bottom, where you're bringing it to life online and offline.

When I did this exercise some years ago – and I haven't found a reason to change it yet – here's what I came up with for the top of the pyramid: "finding and living my own definition of success and helping others do the same". This is what I ultimately want to be known for.

For years, I've had an internal debate as to where I should be focusing. I talk a lot about "escaping the 9 to 5" in the sense of quitting your job and starting your business. I really do believe that this is the best way to get the freedom, flexibility, and fulfilment that so many of us long for. The name of my podcast, however, is Reimagining Success™ and it's this bigger message that I'm most passionate about. I'm not attached to the idea of quitting your job – that's not the point. In fact, I work with many clients who want to establish or build their personal brand within their corporate role, and I also work closely with companies to support their employees. In no way am I trying to persuade people to quit their jobs. So, for me, what I ultimately want to be known for is this overarching mission of "redefining success".

Then in terms of how I bring it to life... I've now been in business for some time, and I certainly didn't have all these things in place when I first started. I had just a couple of headshots that I had taken for my LinkedIn profile and website. I initially commissioned a very cheap logo on Fiverr, which lasted only a few days, and then I commissioned a 'proper' one on 99designs.

Today, I have the business name One Step Outside™ and the dreamcatcher logo, along with professional graphics that I use across my website and social media (and, now, here in this book). I have a set of pictures that includes profile and head shots (where I tend to use the same one consistently, wearing an on-brand and eye-catching yellow top – you'll find it on the back cover) as well as lifestyle images. I have my website headline, translated into a bio for Instagram, LinkedIn, and other social channels. I also have my core concepts of "reimagining success" and "escaping the 9 to 5".

What do you ultimately want to be known for?

To come up with a headline, you'll want to elevate above the specific thing that you're doing just now – interior design, music for weddings, leadership consulting, or whatever service you're currently providing. What is it that you truly care about? What is your bigger purpose? Especially if you have several different businesses in mind, how can you elevate above those ideas to find an 'umbrella theme' to represent you and your individual persona, rather than a specific business? What do these businesses and ideas have in common?

"I help X do Y so that Z."

To translate this into an effective headline, I suggest that you try a proven formula. You can always play around with this as you get more clarity and confidence, but this way you'll make sure that you include the key elements. The formula is, "I help x do y so that z," or "I help [this type of client] achieve [this goal] so that [ultimate end result]." In my case, for example, "I help experienced corporate professionals design a profitable business and a life that gives them more freedom, flexibility and fulfilment."

That last bit, the ultimate result, is the 'so what?' – and this is important. If you're a copywriter, you might say, "I help people write copy." So what? What exactly are you helping them do, and why does it matter? "I help coaches craft more compelling copy that attracts their ideal clients so that they can charge more for their services."

Some more examples from clients of mine…

Valentina at Coco Consulting: *"Helping leaders create inclusive and high performing teams to drive innovation, reduce employee turnover and build high-trust environments."*

Justin at Steady Growth Co: *"Helping driven professionals achieve greater growth, success and fulfilment as technical sales leaders."*

Debbie at Integrity and Grace: *"I help women navigate 'next chapter' moments with clarity, confidence, and calm."*

Vicki at 3J Hunter: *"I help construction companies win work so they can grow."*

Charlotte at Chill and Nourish: *"Helping women with autoimmune conditions nourish their body to prepare to get pregnant naturally."*

Many coaches will say, "I help people achieve their goals", "I help people live their best life," blah, blah, blah. Try to be specific and use language that is meaningful and that you can comfortably use without you, or your audience, cringing.

Your 'headline' or elevator pitch gives you a starting point that you can then translate into different formats, whether you're speaking to someone in person, writing your Instagram bio, or filling in your LinkedIn profile.

How do you want to show up?

Alongside your headline, think about the image that you're portraying. If you're just starting out, I don't want you to overthink this, or feel that you need to invest a lot of money in photographers and graphic designers. However, you will want to have at least a handful of professional pictures of you that you can use on your website, on podcast or media interviews, for your social media profiles, and so on. A simple photo shoot can be very affordable.

For the logo, as I mentioned, I used 99designs to crowdsource the design, and then later an individual graphic designer to help me evolve the brand concept. Personally, I'm a writer and not a designer, so I had to outsource this; of course, if you're more graphically talented than I am, you can consider creating your own. I would even argue that you don't need a logo right away – your name and perhaps a specific font is a perfectly acceptable starting point.

When it comes to colours, people tend to choose these based on their personal preferences. I'll admit that I chose the main coral and teal colours of my brand because I liked them. However, there is psychology behind different colours, and you might want to consider what they each represent and how they work together before you start splashing your favourite pastel pink or neon orange across your website.

So, as the first piece of your personal brand, we're working on really nailing that elevator pitch – anchoring your big picture purpose in a very concrete sentence where you're articulating who you work with and the problem that you solve – and bringing it to life in your colours and imagery.

Exercise 4-1:

1. What do you ultimately want to be known for?
2. What's your elevator pitch? Use the formula, "I help x do y so that z."
   a. Who do you help?
   b. What problem do you solve?
   c. What result do you help them get?

   Put it all together and then practise saying it out loud. If it sounds ridiculous, it might just be down to repetition; or it might be that you need to use more natural language.

CREATING YOUR CONTENT STRATEGY

We've looked at what an effective personal brand can do for you, and we started at the top of my pyramid with your headline or elevator pitch. As powerful as that one sentence can be, it doesn't do much good sitting on your website and social profiles. You need to bring it to life by creating content.

Back in my corporate days, we used to say that "content is king". This was an important swing of the pendulum after years of traditional advertising where you would just sell, sell, sell. However, as Canadian writer and content brand strategist Arjun Basu (2016) puts it…

Without strategy, content is just stuff, and the world has enough stuff.

If you're just putting out a reel or writing a post whenever you feel like it, covering whatever pops into your head… Well, as much as you may value authentic, spontaneous content, it's not going to get you very far. You need to consider the purpose of your content as part of your bigger business and brand strategy, and how this piece of content serves that bigger purpose. What about your audience, what do they care about? What do they need to know and understand before working with you?

I'm a big advocate of a robust content strategy, and this was my area of expertise in the final years of my corporate work. Heading up digital for our premium fragrance, make-up, and skincare department, it was my big focus and contribution. I put content strategy at the forefront of the capability building and training programmes that I developed, partnering with big players like Google and Facebook as well as our media agencies to help brands develop their own strategies.

In the current context of your business and specifically the fourth pillar, the question is: what content are you going to create to bring to life your personal brand? That's also why it's so important to be clear on your personal brand to begin with – to understand what it is that you want to stand for, your values, your skills and strengths, what makes you credible – so that you can then consider how you're going to communicate these elements to the world.

Finding your content sweet spot

While the temptation is to start thinking about content formats and where you're going to be posting, this is the last step in the strategy. The first step is to come up with your content themes. In the past, I would have talked about the sweet spot between two overlapping circles: first, the business or the brand; and second, the ideal client or audience. The sweet spot could be found in content that was both relevant and credible for your brand, and interesting and useful for your target customer.

I would like to now add a third circle into the mix. You have the business brand; the client target; and then you also have you, the business owner. Yes, there is a distinction, even when you are a solopreneur building a business that you love, between your business as an entity and you as an individual.

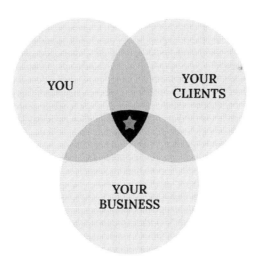

Figure 21: Finding your content sweet spot

For example, I have my business, One Step Outside™; but there is also the human being Anna Lundberg and, believe it or not, these are related but separate things. There are topics that the business will talk about that aren't necessarily a part of my life – for example, because I quit my job many years ago now – and there are also things that are important to me in my personal life that aren't relevant to this business and brand.

With the addition of the third circle, then, you're trying to find the content sweet spot at the intersection of your business, your client target, and you as an individual. A subtle distinction, but I think it's an important one.

To make this more concrete, let me develop my own example a little further. As an individual, my bigger purpose is to reimagine success for myself and help others do the same; I'm location independent, currently living by the sea on the south coast of England; and I'm focused on making my business work for me around my family with two young children.

Next, what do my ideal clients care about? They want to know, "how do I define success?" (although they probably won't use that language), "how do I work out what I want?", "how do I start my own business so that I can quit my job?", "how do I get better work-life balance?", "how do I market myself?" and so on.

Finally, the business wants to talk about the Business Academy course, the Incubator and Accelerator programmes, and my one-to-one coaching.

You can see that there's a different dimension to each of the three areas and there's an overlap in the centre; that overlap is the magic sweet spot where I can create content that serves a purpose.

For me, then, the sweet spot is where I will talk about how to build a life outside the 9 to 5, the 5 Pillars, and specifically redefining success, building your personal brand, and designing your work-life integration. This content is authentic and meaningful to me, my stories, and my experiences; it's relevant and helpful for my ideal clients; and it will serve to grow my business as it feeds into my paid programmes.

The different types of content

If you haven't noticed by now, I love a good framework, and one that we've already touched on and that you may be familiar with is the traditional marketing funnel. In my corporate days, we would have had the following stages:

- **awareness** – at this stage, people are finding out that you exist;
- **consideration** – now, they are beginning to think about buying from you;
- **purchase** – this is where they get out their credit card. In fact, it doesn't end there, because you also have…
- **loyalty and advocacy** – this is when you're interacting with your clients during and after their purchase.

At this point, we could get into the flaws of this old model and look at alternatives. It's true that the actual 'path to purchase' for a customer is unlikely to be this linear, moving through the stages 1-2-3-4. However, rather than get into an intellectual debate on marketing theory, I'm going to keep this model for the sake of simplicity. For our purposes, it serves as a useful representation of how people will enter your ecosystem and ultimately choose to work with you.

For each of the funnel stages, therefore, I've come up with the type of content you need to be developing for the prospect at that stage. I call these the 3Is: Inspire, Instruct, Invite.

- **Inspire** – At this stage, when you're first getting in front of new people, you want to be inspiring them by painting a picture of the big dream, your broader mission and philosophy. In terms of the personal brand framework, this will be your purpose, and your core values; the 'so what?' of your elevator pitch.

- **Instruct** – Once you've attracted the people who resonate with your bigger message, you can start educating them, answering their questions, sharing your frameworks and methodology. This will come from your skills and strengths, and your credibility as an expert, as you demonstrate that you know what you're talking about, and you have a solution for their problem(s).

- **Invite** – Finally, you will need to share the services and programmes that you offer, tell people how they can work with you, and invite them to take action. Here, you'll be talking about the specific results they can expect from working with you, sharing client case studies and testimonials, and giving them clear next steps.

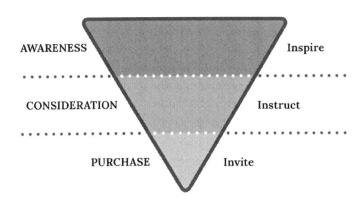

Figure 22: The 3Is of content creation

Let's make this more concrete again with my own business...

- **Inspire** – In my inspirational content, I'll talk about my broader message of reimagining success, escaping the 9 to 5, and creating more freedom, flexibility, and fulfilment. I'll share stories of my own experience, post thoughtful quotes, and express a point of view.

- **Instruct** – In my educational content, I'll share my 5 Pillars framework; I'll write blog posts, record podcast episodes, and run workshops and masterclasses on topics including how to start a business, how to make time for a side hustle, why your personal brand is so important, and how to be more confident as you embark on a career change.

- **Invite** – In the final stage of my content, I'll post each month when I have a spot available for a new one-to-one coaching client; I'll talk about how the Business Academy and Incubator will help experienced professionals transition out of their corporate job and into working for themselves, or how the Accelerator will support existing business owners in getting to the next level of success; and I'll tell people that they can book a free consultation call with me to discuss how I can support them.

The content creation process

We've explored your content sweet spot – the content themes that sit at the overlap of your business, your client, and you as an individual. We've also looked at the three types of content you'll need to create to support each stage of the marketing funnel, the 3Is – Inspire, Instruct, and Invite. Now, we're going to get very practical and look at how you're going to start creating and sharing this content. For that, we have another model.

The 3Ps outline the steps you need to take to bring to life your content strategy: Plan, Produce, Promote.

- **Plan** – The first step is always to plan out your content. You'll start with your content sweet spot and core themes; then, you'll identify the specific topics that your ideal clients want to and need to hear about, and that will feed into your programmes.

- **Produce** – Next, you're going to produce, or create, the content. You'll record your videos and podcast episodes, write your posts, shoot pictures, and create your graphics for social media.

- **Promote** – Finally, you'll post your content, either by scheduling it ahead of time or by posting live on the day, so that people can see the amazing content that you've created.

Figure 23: The 3Ps content workflow

Let me walk you through a specific example from my own business again, to help you see how this comes to life.

- **Plan** – In this first stage, I'll start with the theme. For example, the theme might be personal branding, which of course is Pillar 4 that we're working through now. Under this umbrella theme, I'll come up with specific topics. Each week will then focus on one of those topics, and I'll do, say, a short video introducing the topic on the Monday, a quote on the Tuesday, a 'how to' on the Wednesday, a personal story on the Thursday, and a call to action on the Friday.

- **Produce** – I'm a fan of 'batch creating', which means that I'll block time in my calendar each month to record all the podcast episodes, then block another time slot for filming the videos, and another for writing out the posts.

- **Promote** – The final stage is when my assistant will schedule or post the content live on my website and across the different social channels.

Let's not sugar coat this: this is a lot of work, and it might well seem overwhelming to you at this point. In fact, I'm always looking for ways to strip it back and simplify, while also evolving the strategy as my business and, inevitably, the social media platforms evolve. There is a great deal of discipline and consistency required here.

Remember, however, that those people you see – including me – who are monster creators today will have started with nothing, just like you. You don't have to post five times a day, create 20 videos each week, and cover every single channel right now when you're just beginning. Start small and plan out a schedule that feels realistic and achievable for you; then you can layer new things on as you get into a good rhythm.

Exercise 4-2:

1. Develop themes at your content sweet spot.
    a. What do you want to talk about?
    b. What does your target client want to, or need to, hear about?
    c. What does your business want to talk about?
    Find the patterns and commonalities across the three areas.
2. Start drafting some ideas for the 3Is.
    a. How will you Inspire your audience?

      b. How will you Instruct them?

      c. How will you Invite them to work with you?

3. Have a go at planning out one month of content.

      a. What is your chosen theme?

      b. What will be your four weekly topics?

      c. What is the call to action?

BOOSTING YOUR CREDIBILITY

I've touched on your credibility as an expert a few times already, and I want to go a little deeper here. It really is important when it comes to building your personal brand, especially in a new field, and attracting paying clients. What is it that makes you credible in delivering the results that you're promising?

As I discovered myself when I put up a new website after completing my coach training, declaring, "Hello world, I'm now a coach," does not lead to an immediate influx of coaching clients. People knew me as an expert in digital marketing, branding and content strategy, luxury and beauty – if they knew me at all. Why would they suddenly believe that I was an impactful coach who could help them achieve their personal and professional goals?

Coming back to your personal brand framework, we've already looked at your purpose; you have your values, strengths, and skills from the first pillar; and we've looked at your brand identity and elevator pitch. Now, we come to your credibility.

Here, the most obvious starting point, the 'go-to' for most of you, who have come from an academic and corporate background, will be to resort to your official CV. Traditionally, your professional credibility will indeed come from the prestigious university that you went to, the big-name company where you've been working, and all your formal training, qualifications, and certifications. And, yes, these are part of the picture. However, relying only on these things misses the point and can also make things a bit stressful and intimidating for you when you're breaking away from that past and trying to establish yourself as a different kind of expert without all of these formal accolades.

Embarking on a career change and starting a new business does not, however, mean that you're starting from scratch. Don't think that you have to draw a line through all your achievements and experiences just because you're entering a new field or even just because you're repositioning yourself as an independent coach or consultant. You're not returning to your graduate days of being fresh out of school with no experience to rely on. You still have all your work experience, not to mention hobbies, volunteering, parenting, and a whole host of transferrable skills.

Starting with the basics

Let's start with the basics of 'traditional' sources of credibility, but let's look at these things in a more holistic way. Consider your work experience and go beyond the job title and formal job description. What were the softer skills that you were bringing to the table? What were your achievements that are recognisable as such even outside of your specific role and industry?

What education, training, and certifications do you already have that demonstrate your credibility as a professional in general if not the specific expertise that you're now claiming? If there are gaps, what could you do to fill those gaps? This might be in the form of a formal qualification, especially if it is a legal requirement in your space; but it doesn't have to be.

Although coaching is an unregulated industry, and anyone can say "I'm a coach," I chose to invest in a comprehensive training programme accredited by the official body of the International Coach Federation (ICF). This was for the sake of my own personal development, for my integrity and ethics, and, above all, for my confidence in this new space.

There is also a lot of more informal training and learning that you can do alongside building your business, so that you don't waste time waiting for that magical day (that will never come) when you feel fully qualified and confident to go ahead.

Finally, look back at your references and testimonials. When you're just starting out in your business, you might not have these for your new programme or service. However, your testimonials and references from previous jobs and programmes are still relevant and useful here; they are a testament to your integrity and professionalism. Remember that your personal brand lives above and beyond any specific business.

So, start with the basics of your existing work experience, transferrable skills, formal training and certifications, as well as your references and testimonials. At the same time, know that your credibility doesn't live and die with those traditional credentials.

Getting creative with new content

One of the big advantages of building your own business and developing an effective personal brand is that there are many creative ways in which you can boost your creativity beyond those basic formal experiences and qualifications. You're not applying to a job via an anonymous online platform where there are 200 other candidates. Instead, you have an opportunity to take control and be proactive and creative about building your credibility.

Here, I want to highlight three ways to do this:

- **teach what you know;**
- **develop your own proprietary frameworks; and**
- **create your own platform.**

Let's break these down, one by one.

Teach what you know

The first way in which you can boost your credibility is by teaching what you know. You can do this simply via your social content, by sharing tips and 'how-tos' to demonstrate that you know what you're talking about.

A more in-depth way to do this is to run a workshop or a masterclass. These sessions can be free, or they can be paid, and they are a great way to bring to life your expertise as you walk your audience through your methodology or framework.

A more advanced strategy is to speak at events, either virtual or in person. If you're up on that stage at a conference, on the list of experts at a virtual summit, or being interviewed on someone's podcast, there is a degree of credibility that is automatically earned.

Develop your own proprietary frameworks

The second way of boosting your credibility is to develop your own IP (intellectual property). When you're starting out, you might not have these fully formed yet. If that's the case, as I shared in the business model section, I would encourage you to first work with your clients on a one-to-one basis to validate your thinking and formalise your frameworks as you go.

For example, as I started coaching, I discovered certain common themes. I was walking clients through the steps of setting clear goals, overcoming mindset issues, devising a strategy and a plan... Ultimately, these became what you now recognise as the 5 Pillars, which form the basis of this book as well as much of my free and paid content. The 5 Pillars framework represents the consolidation of my experience and expertise as to how you can build a life outside of the 9 to 5.

Figure 24: The 5 Pillars

So, I teach those pillars. I'll cover them at a high level in my free masterclass, I'll run deep-dive paid workshops, and I'll post content on my social media channels structured around these pillars. I am the only person in the world who is teaching the 5 Pillars and that makes me the definitive expert.

I have other models too. I have the 5Ls, which I introduced you to in Pillar 1, the Live – Love – Learn – Lead – Laugh. I also have my personal brand framework, which we've been using throughout this pillar. And I have more specific models including the 3Is and 3Ps, which we were working through in the previous chapter.

When I talk about proprietary frameworks, I'm not saying that you need to legally protect them, necessarily. I'm not a legal expert so please don't take this as official advice; I'm simply saying that sharing your frameworks and methodologies will demonstrate your expertise, boost your credibility, and establish you as a unique and distinctive expert – whether you have trademarked them formally or not.

Create your own platform

The third and final way in which you can boost your credibility is to create your own platform. This 'platform' can take on different forms, including writing a book, launching a podcast, or even creating a community such as a Facebook group.

Having your own podcast, for example, provides a platform for speaking to other experts, giving you a degree of credibility by association and establishing you as an expert yourself as the host of that podcast.

Being the author of a book gives you a platform for being interviewed on other people's podcasts, or having a feature in a magazine, or speaking at a conference. Everyone knows the hard work that goes into writing a book and it gives you an immediate stamp of credibility (something that I hope you are experiencing as you read this book!).

If publishing your own book seems intimidating to you right now, know that I started by writing little 'eBooks'. These were ten-page Word documents that I turned into PDFs. They were a far cry from the traditionally published full-length business books on the bestseller lists; but they were still powerful content and served the purpose of demonstrating my knowledge. The next level for me was to self-publish *Leaving the Corporate 9 to 5*, which was a collection of interviews with other people who had left their corporate jobs. And, today, you're holding in your hand my 'proper' full-length non-fiction book that's fully based on my own expertise and the 5 Pillars framework.

A book like this can also give you a platform to feed into your paid services and programmes. As a reader, if you want to take your learning further, you can sign up for my 5 Pillars course, the Outsiders Business Academy; and if you want to get comprehensive support in implementing what you're learning, you can choose to work with me as your coach in the Business Incubator or the Accelerator or on a one-to-one basis. (You can read more about these programmes at onestepoutside.com.)

You can see that you can get a lot more creative with how you're building your credibility beyond the basics of traditional work experience and credentials.

Coming back then to my initial, "I'm a coach" declaration as a fresh new graduate… Since then, I have absolutely drawn on the 'traditional' markers of credibility, including my degree from the University of Oxford, my years at Procter & Gamble, and my formal training and certification as an accredited coach. I have then supplemented this by teaching what I know via my social media content, in my paid and free workshops, and in blog posts and media articles. And I have created my own platform in the form of the Reimagining Success™ podcast and now also this book.

What makes you credible in delivering the results you promise? How can you boost that credibility, using the different methods that I've just described? And, with that, you have completed your personal brand framework. I hope you find this framework useful as a visualisation of what you stand for, and that you can use it as a reference as you start to bring it to life in your work.

Exercise 4-3:

1. Map out your experience and formal credentials.
    a. What is your relevant work experience?
    b. What education, qualifications, or certifications do you have?
    c. What references and testimonials can you use from past roles and projects?
    d. Where are the gaps?
2. Consider other ways in which you can boost your credibility.
    a. Where and how can you teach what you know?
    b. What are the steps of your method? What frameworks can you create?
    c. What book(s) might you write, what podcast could you create, to establish yourself as an authority?

MAXIMISING YOUR VISIBILITY

The fourth and final step of Pillar 4, building an effective personal brand, is an important one. It has certainly been a hard lesson for me to learn myself, and I want to help you avoid making the same mistake that I made.

We're talking about maximising your visibility. You will have heard of the TED conferences and their influential talks, and the head of TED, Chris Anderson (quoted in Kukral, 2006) is bound to know a thing or two about personal branding and visibility:

"Your brand isn't what you say it is. It's what Google says it is."

It's all very well for me to develop a personal brand strategy on a nice piece of paper, create a beautiful website, or publish a load of content on Instagram, but it doesn't matter one bit if nobody sees it.

This is not just about search engine optimisation (SEO), although that can be a part of it. If someone Googles you and they find unrelated content from your personal Facebook profile or, perhaps worse, they don't find you at all – well, that is how they'll see you. Your current online presence most likely does not reflect where you want your personal brand to be, especially now that you're moving into a new space and after you've done all this in-depth strategic work on your personal brand framework.

Visibility is about getting in front of the right people with the right message at the right time. In a way, that's what marketing is all about. It's very tempting, however – and this is the mistake that I made in the past and sometimes still get sucked into – to spend hours and hours perfecting your content and then getting disappointed when it doesn't 'go viral'. Posting something once, on one channel, and hoping everyone will see it is not an effective strategy. You can have the most beautiful and professionally crafted posts, graphics, and videos, but, again, it doesn't matter if nobody ever sees them.

What do people see?

To illustrate this, let's look at what people see of your personal brand. We start with the big picture of who you are – your mission, your core values and beliefs, your skills and strengths, and your professional and personal experience.

As we know, there is a line between who you are as a human being, the 'whole' you as it were, and who you are as a business owner. Your personal brand is a curated image, so you're only sharing a part of who you are at any given time. You're telling stories, walking people through your frameworks, and promoting your products and services.

Ultimately, your prospects will only ever see a tiny part of that. They'll see your visual brand identity and then they'll see a small number of your posts or emails or articles that you're producing.

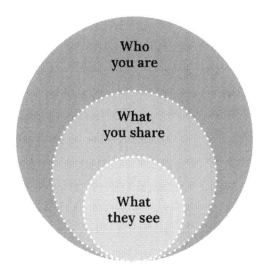

Figure 25: What do people see?

I've seen various numbers over the years as to how many times a consumer or prospect needs to have interacted with you to buy from you. A 'touchpoint' where someone interacts with you might be seeing a post on social, watching a short video, joining a workshop, or even having an email exchange with you. In the past, I think the number was 7; then I saw 13; I've even seen 25.

So, look, there are people, and I've had people in the past, who do a search on Google or LinkedIn, find your profile, book a call and then, BOOM, they make the payment, and you start working together. That's the dream; but it doesn't always happen that way…

At the other end of the spectrum and, again, I've had this happen too, you can have people who will watch you from afar over the span of years before finally putting up their hand and choosing to work with you. Most prospects will probably fall in between these two extremes.

The most common scenario, and therefore the way in which I've designed my materials and the customer journey, is something like this… An ideal client might see a short video on Instagram, the message will resonate, and they'll click through to my profile. There they'll see my highlighted posts and, if they like what they see, they might follow me. After they do so, they'll start seeing more of my content. At some point, they might follow a call to action in one of my posts asking them to download my free 5 Pillars scorecard. They'll click onto the link (onestepoutside.com/scorecard), enter their name and email address, and download the resource.

After that, they'll get an initial warm-up email sequence, where I'll tell them more of my story, give them more context on the 5 Pillars, and go into how I can help them build that life outside the 9 to 5. After the welcome sequence, they'll continue to get my weekly email where I share the latest podcast episode, give additional insights, and promote one of my workshops.

If the topic is relevant, they'll sign up and join the live session, where they'll learn more about my approach and get a feel for my style. They'll reflect on how they could get even better results by working with me directly, they'll book a consultation, and I'll propose the best programme for them. Then, if they're convinced by the offer, they'll make the investment. PHEW.

You can see from this example why you have the whole ecosystem that we looked at in the previous pillar. It's not a linear process, people aren't going to necessarily follow the exact path that I've laid out, and it might take them a long time. However, I'm giving people these different entry points, ways to discover who I am, to get to know me and learn from me and, ultimately, how we can work together.

This is where visibility comes into play. If this theoretical prospect hadn't seen my video appear in their feed, for example, it wouldn't matter how pretty my Instagram profile was. My LinkedIn profile can be incredibly effective and compelling but if I never appear in the prospect's news feed, if nobody ever mentions me and I never comment or engage with other people's content, then they're not going to ever see that profile. I can have the most incredible frameworks and services and solutions, but I'll remain the best-kept secret in the industry, and I'll never grow my business and my impact, if I'm not consistently visible.

Choosing your channels

Do you remember how I said that the temptation with content is to jump straight to the formats and channels? Well, having found your content sweet spot, planned different types of content, and looked at ways to boost your credibility, we've finally arrived at this last step. Now that you have your content themes and topics, you can choose the channels where you are going to distribute and promote the content that you're creating.

To make that decision, ask yourself three questions:

- **Where are your ideal clients active?**
- **Where do you enjoy spending time?**
- **Which channels are appropriate for the topic?**

So, first, where are your ideal clients active? Are they CEOs, executives, or business owners who are likely to be active on LinkedIn? Are they perhaps smaller creative business owners who spend their time on Instagram? It's not just social media we're talking about here; you can also consider the magazines that they're reading, events they're going to, and podcasts they're listening to.

It's not just about where your clients are active, however. As ever, you want to make sure that this is a business that you will love and that you will want to stick to your plan with the discipline that is required to get consistent results. So, you also need to ask yourself, where do you enjoy spending your time?

I'll often hear clients moan and groan about, "Oh, I hate Facebook," "I can't bear the thought of all that dancing on Instagram," "I'm too old for TikTok…" The thing is: you don't have to do any of those things. You're designing and building a business that works for you, which means one that fits your practical parameters but also your personal preferences and bigger purpose. Remember your criteria from the business model, Pillar 3? Where do you want to show up?

Finally, you need to ask yourself, which channels are appropriate for the topic? At the time of writing, there are complaints that LinkedIn is becoming more like Facebook, and there is also a lot of copying going on between different channels as their features become more and more alike. As a simple example, though, if you're talking about talent development or leadership coaching, then LinkedIn is an obvious place to start; as are learning and development conferences, and relevant industry magazines. If the topic is health and nutrition, weight loss, or couples therapy, perhaps Instagram might be a better fit, along with publications and blogs on these wellness topics.

Again, we're not just talking about social media. With my background in digital marketing, I must admit that this is my 'go-to' but there are so many other channels that can supplement a social media strategy and might be a more effective and enjoyable strategy for you.

As a writer, I know that pitching my articles and expertise to relevant magazines and publications is a great way to get in front of new audiences. Likewise, speaking at conferences puts you up there on stage as an expert, but even attending a conference and chatting to people in the coffee area can be a great way to connect with new people.

Think beyond social media and screen time to consider where your prospects are active physically, what events and conferences and workshops they are going to, what podcasts they're listening to, and what magazines and newspapers they are reading.

Choosing your formats

Okay, so you've got your channels; you also need to look at the formats. Some channels require a certain format – YouTube, for example, requires you to produce videos – while others are more flexible. Here, again, you'll want to remember your criteria and your preferences.

Writing was always my first love and a natural skill, and so my first choice has been to write blog articles, publish written posts and email newsletters, and pitch my articles to the media. I've also found that I enjoy speaking, thanks perhaps to my years of amateur theatre, and so this has led to my podcast, short- and long-form videos, keynotes, and workshops. Audio podcasts and virtual presentations have been a particular favourite for me, as they are easy to do from home without a long commute and other logistical complexities. Live videos were a godsend as they disrupted my perfectionist tendencies of wanting to endlessly re-record my videos and forced me to just show up in the moment. And, as my hunger for more personal connection grows, I'm considering more in-person events and opportunities to engage IRL (in real life).

Are you an avid writer like me? Then written posts and articles are a good place to start. Perhaps you're more of a visual person, a designer, a photographer, an illustrator? Creating cartoons, infographics, or beautiful imagery might be the way to go. What are you good at, and what do you enjoy?

Video is a great way to connect with your audience and build credibility; but perhaps you feel nervous about getting on camera? There is an element of having to get out of your comfort zone and learning how to feel more confident on video. On the other hand, if you really hate the idea and don't think you'll ever come to terms with recording videos, then this is probably not going to be the best primary format for you.

You do also want to consider the other side of the equation, which is how your prospects and clients want to learn, and how you can best bring to life the messages that you're trying to convey. If your ideal client is a super busy senior corporate executive who's also a parent to young children, then maybe you can create a short 15-minute podcast series, like mine, where they can listen on the commute to work or while they're hanging up the laundry? If yours is a more complex topic, and you have an academic audience of intellectuals who really want to go deep, then perhaps longer-form technical content is more appropriate. Is it a young target that just wants a 30-second reel or a short voice note, or an older more traditional audience that wants a formal presentation?

Again, the answers lie in that sweet spot between what you want to do personally, what your target client wants, and what will best serve your business.

Repurposing your content

In this context of maximising your visibility, I started out by saying that you can't just post something once and then be done with it. I've also acknowledged that all this content creation can be overwhelming. The good news is that there is a solution here, and that is repurposing your content.

What does this mean? Well, remember the 3Ps, the Plan – Produce – Promote? Let's say, in this case, that I'm focusing on my second pillar, which is cultivating your confidence and resilience. I then have a weekly topic, for example, how to embrace a growth mindset. I will do a podcast episode, which then sits on the website along with a transcript; I will do a short video introducing the topic at the start of the week; and I'll create posts on Instagram, Facebook, and LinkedIn with text and visuals drawn from the podcast episode transcript. So, over the course of the week, I'll have one theme and one topic and then create content that will be distributed across my different channels in all sorts of different formats.

Remember also the 7, 13, or 25 touchpoints: most people won't even see your post the first time, and they might not have time to listen to the podcast episode when it first comes out or watch the video right away. Repurposing allows different people to consume your content in different ways, while making it more likely that a given person will see the message (and, ideally, take the action you want them to take).

Beyond this weekly rhythm, we've also been reposting posts 'from the archive' in my Facebook group, sharing past content that is very relevant to the new topic that week. This archive consists of more than 200 podcast episodes at the time of writing, along with blog posts and other resources. It's all valuable content that existing people need to see more than once, and new people entering the ecosystem still need to see for the first time.

To hammer this point home, I've seen suggestions that you spend 20% of your time on creating a piece of content, and 80% on amplifying it so that people see it. Whether this is the exact split or not, the intention, I think, is right: make sure that you're thinking seriously about getting your content out there and being consumed once you've invested your valuable time in creating it.

Having more conversations

I have a couple more 'hacks' for you, that are particularly useful for you when you're first starting out. If you're right at the beginning of the process and you don't yet have the confidence or the discipline to create lots of original content every week, there is another way.

Start by interacting with other people, engaging, commenting, and having more conversations. In fact, I would even argue that this can be more effective than publishing your original content on your channels because you are having real conversations with real people. That means that you're appearing in their feeds and getting new 'eyeballs', as we call them in marketing, on your ideas.

Let's say that you've chosen B2B, Business to Business, as the core of your business model. You've identified your wish list of companies that you want to work with, and you've connected with the relevant people within those companies on LinkedIn. If you now start interacting on their posts, leaving a thoughtful comment, sharing relevant articles from industry publications, and perhaps tagging someone to say, "I'd love to get your perspective…" this will do wonders for your credibility and visibility. You'll start appearing in the feed and, as your name pops up again and again, you'll be increasing those all-important touch points and placing yourself top of mind as an expert in your field when the time comes for these companies to consider working with you.

Have a think about what are the main topics, companies, and figures that you want to be following and engaging with. In addition to your B2B wish list of companies, who are the public figures who cover complementary topics for a similar audience?

In my case, I might consider experts and influencers in work-life balance, hybrid working, finding your purpose, setting meaningful goals, juggling motherhood with career, overcoming imposter syndrome… I'll follow, for example, Arianna Huffington, who is an advocate for finding a different metric of success, the importance of taking care of yourself and, specifically, sleep.

If you want to take this strategy seriously, you can block out time in your calendar every morning, let's say, to tap into industry news and engage with stakeholders on LinkedIn, to comment and DM people on Instagram, and to interact on whichever channels you have chosen for your business. Consider following specific hashtags and signing up to Google Alerts to get relevant topics and articles to share.

Leveraging other people's audiences

The next 'hack' is also great when you're starting out and an effective strategy for getting in front of new people in the longer term. Your own podcast can be a fantastic platform for you, but the truth is that there's a lot of work that goes into recording a podcast, editing it, and promoting it. The same goes for creating your own Facebook group and community or running your own virtual summit. Not only do these things involve a lot of work, but they are also very slow in terms of getting results at the beginning as you won't have the audience to get the traction that you want. It's much smarter, then, to leverage other people's existing audiences.

Rather than (or, at least, as well as) launching your own podcast, consider pitching yourself to appear on other people's podcasts. Don't be like those misguided souls who blindly send generic messages to any podcast without first checking if it's a fit, or if they even take guests. Instead, take the time to identify podcasts where there is a synergy in terms of your topic or audience, without being competitors.

In my case, I have a few different angles to consider. As a business mentor, I can come on and focus on how to choose the right business model or how to build your personal brand; as a mother, I can talk about being a 'mumpreneur'; and my 'reimagining success' message can be relevant for a whole range of different podcasts.

Create a list of possible podcasts and take the time to send a thoughtful email or message with supporting information on why you think you'd be a good fit and the value you could bring to their audience. Do the same with other experts who are running virtual summits or retreats where they need collaborators; bloggers and online publications; and perhaps also traditional print media.

For podcasts, for example, you can look at the top 100 on Apple Podcasts in your category, or you can search by keywords. I'd recommend that you have a mix of the big influencers – the Arianna Huffingtons, Brené Browns, and

Steven Bartletts of the world – alongside smaller players. Many of the podcasts that I've been on have been run by coaches and experts who were new to the field and certainly new to podcasting. Even a small audience is still an audience, and each podcast episode or article can get you one or two new people coming into your ecosystem. Plus, you never know where these early-stage influencers will grow to in the future.

Piggy backing on someone else's platform to speak to their audience is also a great way to consolidate and clarify your positioning, as you refine what it is you're saying each time. Give the audience a clear call to action to come over to your podcast, to download a free resource, or to book a call with you – and that's how you'll bring these new people into your ecosystem.

Exercise 4-4:

1. Choose 2-3 channels where you want to be present. Consider where your clients are active, where you enjoy spending your time, and what is appropriate for your business.
2. Decide on your primary format and then map out how you can repurpose your content into other formats.
3. What are the main topics, companies, and public figures that you want to follow and engage with?
4. What kind of podcasts, publications, and businesses might you collaborate with or contribute to in order to get in front of a relevant audience?

Pillar 5:
Designing flexible work-life integration

PILLAR 5:
DESIGNING FLEXIBLE WORK-LIFE INTEGRATION

We've arrived at the final pillar, Pillar 5: designing flexible work life-integration. In a way, we're coming back full circle to Pillar 1 and your definition of success. Remember the balance that you're trying to achieve across the different areas of your life? Now we're getting more concrete as we dig into how you can plan and structure your life to bring that big-picture vision to life in your day-to-day habits and routines.

I know that the idea of routine and structure might be abhorrent to you as you rebel against the very rigid 'corporate 9 to 5' that you're escaping from. However, trust me on this, a little bit of structure is what's going to give you the very freedom, flexibility, and fulfilment that you crave.

Before we get into the practical details, however, I want to touch on the broader concept of work-life integration itself. You're most likely more familiar with the idea of work-life *balance*, and I want to explain why I prefer the term *integration*.

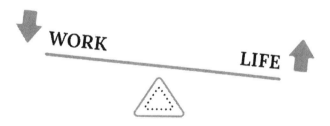

Figure 26: The fallacy of work-life balance

The popular phrase 'work-life balance' creates a false dichotomy, in my view, between 'work' on the one hand and 'life' on the other. You immediately visualise a set of scales (in

French, literally, *une balance*), where you are trying to create an equilibrium between your career or job on the one side and your personal life on the other. More life means less work (and, therefore, less 'success'), and vice versa. As you'll know by now (and as I've demonstrated in my 5Ls model, where we consider the five areas of wellbeing, relationships, learning, career, and fun), work is a part of life. It's not something that's separate, that you can juxtapose with 'life' on the other side.

The reality is so much more complex. Within your personal life, there is family, friendship, hobbies and 'extracurricular' activities, travel, and things like 'life admin' and personal development. You might be making an impact in your personal life through volunteering, for example. You might have a side hustle and other income streams outside of your day job. Within work, there is more going on than just getting paid. You have relationships at work, it affects your mental and physical wellbeing, and, yes, you might even have fun in the office(!).

I prefer 'work-life integration'. Ready access to the internet now means that you can check your emails on your laptop or on your phone and effectively work from anywhere. If this leads to you being 'always on' and never taking a break, that's not such a positive development. If, on the other hand, being able to work after hours at home means that you can use part of your working day to go to the gym, pick up your son from school, or meet your sister for lunch – well, that becomes more attractive.

The beauty of designing your own business, which is what you're doing here, is that you can fully embrace this idea of work-life integration. You no longer need to follow the traditional Monday-to-Friday, 9-to-5, routine; you can break free from that rigid construct and embrace flexibility. You are now choosing to build a career and a lifestyle that you'd be happy to maintain for the rest of your life, and you can get creative with designing solutions that work for you.

Above all, integration means striving for harmony between the different areas of your life, rather than accepting a trade-off. I don't subscribe to the view that being a successful high achiever at work means that you must sacrifice time with your family, or your own health; or that prioritising your children and your wellbeing means giving up on your professional ambitions. There are synergies between these different areas; they are not in competition.

The first step in designing this integration is to get really clear on your priorities. This means knowing what's important from a big picture perspective as well as being clear on the priorities within your business. What are the things that need to be on your calendar every day, every week, for you to reach your goals and make your business, and your life, work for you?

Next, we'll be looking at setting boundaries. It's all very well to have ambitious goals and ideas about what you want your life to look like. If you can't set clear boundaries, if you can't say "no" to make space for the right "yes", well, you're simply never going to get there. In talking about integration between work and life, I'm not advocating for blurring the lines completely; this is not about working in bed, on your holidays, while at the park with your children… There is still a line to be drawn – and you get to choose where you draw that line.

Then we'll be looking at systems. We'll consider the operational processes and tools that are going to simplify, streamline, and automate your work. It might not be the sexiest of topics, however, these systems will allow you to focus on the things that really matter and the things that you love doing, and that will make all the difference for you and your clients.

Finally, we'll be exploring how important it is to learn to delegate and outsource work in certain parts of your business. The kind of business that we're talking about here is generally not a company with physical offices and 50 people on the payroll; rather, we're talking about using assistants, freelancers, perhaps associates, in a way that's going to help you focus on what you really want to, and should, be doing.

Let's do this. The final pillar – stick with me – is Pillar 5, designing flexible work-life integration.

GETTING CLEAR ON YOUR PRIORITIES

The first step in designing flexible work-life integration is getting clear on your priorities. If you don't know what your priorities are, then how on earth are you going to prioritise them? Deceptively simple and yet surprisingly easy to miss.

The word 'priority' has its origins in the Old French *priorite,* Medieval Latin *prioritatem,* and Latin, *prior.* It initially meant first or prior in the sense of time, and later first in rank or order. As such, there could only be one priority. It's only more recently that we've pluralised priority to create multiple priorities and, in doing so, we've rendered it largely meaningless.

When we agreed our work plans with our line manager in my early marketing roles, we would allocate the priority 1, 2 or 3. Inevitably, we would make all the projects priority 1. However, if everything is a priority, then nothing is a priority. You really do need to come back to those more historical definitions of the word and have a clear idea of what one thing needs to come first.

To help you get clear on this, on what needs to come first, I want to introduce a few concepts to you. First up, we're looking at juggling those balls…

Glass, rubber, and lead

> *Imagine life as a game in which you are juggling some five balls in the air. You name them – work, family, health, friends and spirit – and you're keeping all of these in the air. You will soon understand that work is a rubber ball. If you drop it, it will bounce back. But the other four balls – family, health, friends and spirit – are made of glass. If you drop one of these, they will be irrevocably scuffed, marked, nicked, damaged or even shattered. They will never be the same. You must understand that and strive for balance in your life.*

This was the insight that the former CEO and President of Coca-Cola, Brian Dyson, included in his commencement speech at Georgia Tech in 1991 (and let's just ignore the fact that he used the word 'balance'!). While the idea of juggling balls may be a cliché, it's one that has persisted precisely because it so accurately depicts the experience of life. The nuance that Dyson brings here is that there are different types of balls that you are juggling, and you need to get clear on which ball is which.

There are areas of your life that are rubber balls. When you 'drop the ball' in these areas, that ball will bounce right back up. For example, if I don't post on Instagram, if I stop doing reels, if I don't answer emails for a couple of days... my business is not going to collapse. Yes, if I neglect marketing altogether and if I don't respond to prospects and clients over the longer term, then my business will absolutely suffer. In the meantime, however, as long as I come back to them in due course, I'll be able to bring them back to life.

(At this point, I'm going to diverge and, without wanting to confuse the metaphor, introduce the image of spinning plates. We went to a school fair not long ago and the circus artist there had a final act that she had been working hard on, where she tried to keep eight plates spinning. Each plate needed a lot of concentration and focus at first to get it spinning, but then she could leave it for a while to give the other plates more attention, and the initial plate would maintain its momentum and continue spinning. If she neglected a plate for too long, however, it would come crashing down onto the ground. In an very apt reflection of real life, she never quite succeeded in getting all eight spinning.)

There are other balls in your life that are glass balls. When you drop these, they will shatter into a million pieces. If I'm not eating well, if I don't exercise, if I sleep badly, if I neglect my partner – or, worse, my young children – then my health and personal relationships will suffer. These things are not going to just bounce back up again; they will be damaged, perhaps for good. It's important to be clear on which of your balls are made of rubber, and which are made of glass.

Now, I want to build on this idea further to add a third type of ball. This one is inspired by one of my clients, and I've called it the lead ball. These are balls that you're carrying around with you, obligations, to-dos, 'shoulds', that feel heavy. When you drop them, they'll land on the ground with a thud and you'll immediately feel a sense of relief. You'll find that you can leave these lead balls on the ground, and there's no need to pick them back up again at all. Hurrah.

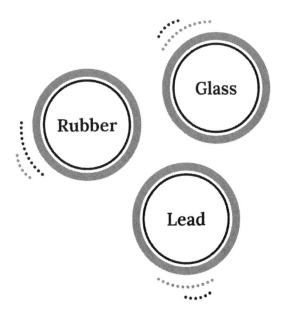

Figure 27: Juggling your balls

The 5 big rocks

Okay, we've looked at balls, and plates, now let's talk about rocks. This concept I believe was at least brought into the mainstream by management guru Stephen Covey (2020), the author of *The 7 Habits of Highly Effective People*. I came across it in one of my very first 'lunch-and-learn' sessions at Procter & Gamble.

Let's imagine that you have an empty jar. Next to it, you have piles of different materials. You have big rocks, medium-sized stones, smaller pebbles, bits of gravel, and some sand. If you can picture the sequence of first pouring in the sand, the gravel, the pebbles, and stones – well, the jar is now quite full. If you then try to put the big rocks in, you can't push them in, and they'll remain on the table.

Let's now reverse the sequence and put the big rocks into the empty jar first. You can place the smaller stones and pebbles in the gaps, and pour in the gravel and the sand... Now, suddenly, you've managed to fit everything – or, at least, the biggest, most important, things – into that same jar.

Figure 28: Putting your big rocks first

The smaller pebbles, the gravel, and the sand – these represent all your admin, the emails and, let's be honest, most of the tasks currently clogging up your to-do list. These things will get done no matter what, they will fit in around your other priorities – and, if they don't, the world is probably not going to end.

The big rocks, on the other hand, are the things that are important, that will make the biggest difference, and that you won't have time for unless you put them first. Within the work and business domain, your big rocks might include writing a book, launching a podcast, or developing a new programme. Taking a step back and looking at your life, your big rocks will probably coincide with your glass balls and will include your family, your health, and maybe a personal passion project.

Knowing what your big rocks are, in life and in business, means that you can literally put them first into your jar, or rather, onto your calendar. We did a lot of work on clarifying what matters from a big picture perspective in the first pillar, so you can refer to that. Your 'big rocks' might represent the 5Ls (Live – Love – Learn – Lead – Laugh); you might choose five roles in your life (I'm a mother, partner, business owner…); or you might choose your five core values.

Now, let's dig into what the big rocks are within your business…

The 5 priorities in your business

This is a framework that I came up with for my Business Accelerator clients, and it's now the framework that guides my priorities in my business on a weekly basis.

You might hear people talk about working 'on' your business – making time for business development and strategy for the future – rather than just doing the busy work of working 'in' your business – focusing only on the day-to-day operational tasks and duties (and I believe this one came from Michael Gerber (2001) in *The E-Myth Revisited*). If you only work *in* the business, you'll never grow and evolve as a business or as an individual.

Taking this idea further, I've identified five different areas where you need to be spending time to build a successful business. These areas are:

- **Income** – these are the activities that will generate a revenue for the business;
- **Visibility** – this is where you're creating and amplifying your content;
- **Service** – here, you're actually delivering the service to your customers;

- **Operations** – these are the behind-the-scenes activities that need to happen for the front-end to work; and
- **Legacy** – these projects are connected to your purpose and will create a lasting impact for you and your clients.

Let me make this more tangible with some examples from my own business. If I start with Income, this is effectively the 'selling' part of my business. I might be doing a free consultation call or running a workshop that will feed into one of my paid programmes. I might be developing a new programme, such as my Business Academy course, as another income stream. I might be posting an invitation on social media, or even better having a direct conversation with people in the private messages to nurture prospects, some of whom will ultimately become paying clients. These are activities that, while not guaranteed to do so, are designed to generate an income.

The second level is Visibility. Here, I might be working on my content calendar, recording videos and podcast episodes, and going live on different social channels. I might also be pitching myself as a guest on other podcasts or pitching myself to the media either as an expert or as a writer. Anything that gets me in front of a new or existing audience so that they get to 'know, like, and trust' me comes under this heading of Visibility.

The third level is Service, which is delivering the service that people are paying for. In simple terms, it involves things like showing up to coaching calls, replying to client emails and messages, or delivering a paid speech or workshop. It also involves anything I can do to improve the quality of the service that I'm delivering. I might be recording training content, creating new worksheets, or coming up with ideas for how I can help my clients get better results, faster.

The fourth level is Operations. These are the kind of things that are important but usually not urgent (at least, not yet). They will include accounting and admin, all the back-end website development and fixes, creating and improving your systems, managing your team behind the scenes, and so on. Last year, for example, I had my main website redesigned, and this year, I updated the private membership site. I've also been reviewing and reducing my expenses, to make sure that the business is as efficient and profitable as possible.

The fifth and highest level of the pyramid is Legacy. This one is the hardest to pin down but also the one that's most closely connected to your purpose, and to creating a fulfilling business that allows you to make a lasting impact. For me, it's realised largely through my books, like this one – more tangible and enduring than all those transient social media posts.

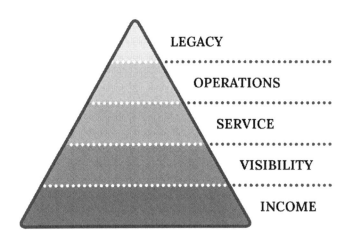

Figure 29: Prioritising your business tasks

It's my thesis that you need to have all five of these things on your calendar to create a successful business, that is, a business that is financially viable, as well as fulfilling and enjoyable for you. However, since this chapter is about priorities, it's worth exploring when one category might be more important than other.

For this, you need to ask yourself, what is your priority right now? Is it delivering the most incredible service to your current clients, as you've launched a new programme and you want to validate the concept and get glowing testimonials that will allow you to go out and sell the service to more people? Is it getting in front of as many new people as possible, as you have no audience yet and no leads coming in and you need people to first know that you exist? Or is it making pragmatic choices that don't necessarily line up completely with your future vision but, with the balance in your bank account quickly diminishing, you really need to urgently bring in an income? (I always tell my clients, "Be optimistic and even idealistic in the long term but be pragmatic in the short term".)

Of the five areas, there are two that often get deprioritised. The first is Operations. If you spend too much time on your back-end tasks, then you're missing an opportunity to be visible and generate sales. On the other hand, clearly, if you neglect your accounting, website updates, and general admin over the longer term, you're going to run into all sorts of problems. Having a time block on your calendar for these tasks (and we'll look at time blocking next) will ensure that you get them done on a regular basis without getting bogged down.

The second area that often gets deprioritised, a true 'big rock' that won't happen unless you put it first, is the Legacy area. This book would never have been written if I hadn't blocked time on my calendar each week to work on it. Yes, there will always be more immediate tasks to distract my attention, and there might be fires that need putting out immediately. However, if I keep carving out that little bit of time and sit down at my computer, if not all then most, Thursday mornings, then I will make progress and, eventually… well, you're holding the result in your hands.

Planning your ideal week

Now to a framework, a tool, that I've been using myself and that I've been recommending to clients for many years. The 'ideal week' involves blocking time on your calendar to reflect the priorities that you have identified. In other words, it's a way in which you can ensure that you are putting first the things that you say you want to put first.

	MONDAY	TUESDAY	WEDNESDAY	THURSDAY	FRIDAY	SATURDAY	SUNDAY
5-6							
6-7							
7-8							
8-9							
9-10							
10-11							
11-12							
12-13							
13-14							
14-15							
15-16							
16-17							
17-18							
18-19							
19-20							
20-21							
21-22							
22-23							
23-00							

Figure 30: Planning your ideal week

When I talk about time blocking and scheduling, a lot of people will initially be reluctant. Especially if you're a creative soul, a 'go-with-the-flow' kind of person, or if you're simply fed up after years of conforming to the rigidity of school and work schedules, you may not be so excited about creating another strict routine now that you're supposed to be 'free'.

Let me first reassure you that this is a *flexible* framework to guide you rather than limit you. Second, I want to try to convince you that a little bit of structure is what creates the freedom that you so long for. Especially if you've quit your job and you suddenly have whole days and weeks stretching out in front of you, it's important to have that structure. It's not efficient to just sit down at your desk, "Right, I need to work on really important things now." If, instead, you're clear that "Okay, it's Monday morning and my first priority is always to respond to messages from my clients and then to continue nurturing conversations with my warm leads," then you can get straight to work on those priorities and use your time effectively.

The ideal week is exactly that, your *ideal* week; you're never going to live it 100%. The intent is to create a plan that guides the reality of your day-to-day routine so that it reflects the big vision you have for your life and business. You're going to block out what you want to be doing, and when, including not just business but all priorities in your life.

First, you can use the 5Ls – you can block, in different colours if you want to get fancy, your Live, Love, Learn, Lead, and Laugh activities. This is a visual way to represent what's important to you and to see right away if there is an imbalance, for example, if there's too much of one colour and not enough of another.

Second, you can 'double click' on the Lead category, and use those five priority categories that we've just been through. You can label activities as to whether they are related to Income, Visibility, Service, Operations, or Legacy.

Once you've mapped out your ideal week, pull up your calendar and see what the reality of today looks like. The two weeks might not be as different as you expected; or, perhaps, your ideal week is a far cry from where you are today. If it's the latter case, it might be that your ideal week is too idealistic. It might also be good news in the sense that if you're not getting the results that you want, there are clear changes you can make as to how you're spending your time.

Again, it's your ideal week, and it's never going to accurately reflect your reality. However, if you get into the routine of planning out your week ahead of time, and then reviewing how it's gone after the fact, you'll have real clarity on whether you're spending your time on the right things. You'll also be able to adjust – either by tweaking the ideal week itself, because you've discovered it doesn't work in practical terms, or by making sure that you show more discipline in sticking to the plan.

Eating the frog

Finally, one more framework, or an idea really, but a powerful one. This one is from productivity consultant Brian Tracy (2013) and his eponymous book, *Eat that Frog*.

We talked about 'priority' in the singular, that there is only ever one priority, one thing that must come prior. This one thing is your 'frog'; it's your biggest, most important project or task. It's the one that you would rather put off and procrastinate on, perhaps because it seems so overwhelming; but it's also the one that would bring you the most income, fulfilment, joy... Whether it's working on your book or sending off a comprehensive proposal to a new client, you need to prioritise this task first thing, before you do anything else. In doing so, you are ensuring that you're creating movement in your business and not just ticking off busy work on your to-do list.

In a way, this is about taking your glass ball, your big rock, your top business priority, and making sure you put that before anything else in your day. Eat the frog first thing. The rest will still get done and, if not, then at least you can be confident in the knowledge that you prioritised what really matters. You will have eaten that frog.

Exercise 5-1:

1. Get clear on your different balls that you're juggling:
   a. glass balls – these will shatter when dropped;
   b. rubber balls – they'll bounce right back; and
   c. lead balls – they are an unnecessary burden.
2. Identify your 'big rocks' that need to go in before all the other stones, pebbles, and sand in your life.
3. Start listing the important tasks that need to get done at this stage of your business. Consider the 5 categories:

a. Income
b. Visibility
c. Service
d. Operations
e. Legacy

Taking all this into consideration, block out your ideal week. Make sure you're incorporating the different areas of your life, and the different priorities in your business. Review and adjust as necessary.

SETTING HEALTHY BOUNDARIES

Okay, so you have your priorities clear, both when it comes to your business and your life. Now, you need to set boundaries to help you stick to those priorities.

Here, I'll call on another super-successful person who is widely quoted to support my point, American business magnate and investor, Warren Buffett (source unknown):

> *The difference between successful people and really successful people is that really successful people say no to almost everything.*

Setting boundaries is closely linked with your priorities. It's about saying "no" to the wrong things, so that you make space for a more important "yes". You're saying "no" both to other people and to other projects, to be able to say "yes" to your bigger purpose, your legacy work, and your big rocks.

This idea of boundaries is critical. To understand why it's so important, you need only ask yourself what happens when you don't have boundaries. You say "yes", even when internally, it's a "no". You end up feeling resentful because you do things you don't want to do, just because you felt you couldn't say "no". This is how your schedule fills up with busy work that isn't necessarily connected to your bigger priorities. And, because of taking on too much, you will probably have to break another commitment and so let someone else down. The ultimate consequence, of course, can also be burnout, with far too much on your plate.

Have a think about what the consequences have been in the past for you, from not having set firm boundaries. Specifically, if you've already been working for yourself for a while, where has this been an issue for you? And what could happen in the future if you continue without setting boundaries? If you don't tell your clients that you're not available in the evenings or that you can't reply at the weekends, for example? Spend some time exploring the negatives to help you recognise the importance of setting, and enforcing, these boundaries.

Identifying your boundaries

The first step has to be to identify what your boundaries are; as ever, you need to define 'success' for you in this space. So, knowing your priorities from the previous chapter, and then knowing what your corresponding boundaries need to be.

It's not enough that you know what your boundaries are, however. You need to tell your partner; perhaps you need to tell the kids, if they're old enough to understand; you need to tell your clients and write them into your terms and conditions. You must communicate clearly what the boundaries are up front, to make it easy to then say, "As we discussed in our first call," or "As we established in our agreement…"

Now, it's not a very nice experience, for you or for your clients, to keep having to tell them, "Please see my Terms and Conditions." I'd encourage you to communicate them clearly and in a 'consumer-friendly' way. If these boundaries are core to how you are going to be doing business together, then it's important that you have those conversations explicitly and early on so that expectations are set and there is no confusion.

Finally, you'll need to enforce the boundaries that you've set and communicated. It's not enough just to say, "Hey, these are my boundaries." You'll need to learn to say "no" when someone tries to overstep a boundary. I know, it's uncomfortable; but you must hold your ground.

For example, if a client says, "Can I do a call on Friday afternoon?" I will say, "I don't take client calls on Friday; I can do Monday, how is that for you?" It's completely up to you what you say, and how much you disclose as to the reason. In my case, I'm being a role model for my clients, showing them that I'm building a business that works with my lifestyle, with my preferences, and so on. I trust that my clients will respect this precisely because they aspire to do the same.

Likewise, I hope you have identified ideal clients who share your values and who will respect your boundaries. You may remember that this was one of the criteria in the client checklist in Pillar 3.

Now, I'd like to break this down into a more granular approach, to come at this from a few different angles. We're going to look at five types of boundaries:

- **physical boundaries;**
- **time boundaries;**
- **emotional boundaries;**
- **communication boundaries; and**
- **your personal, individual, boundaries**.

First, then, what are your physical boundaries? Is your study a sacred space where you don't want kids to come in, and so you shut and lock the door when you've finished working? Do you have a clearly defined working space, and you never work in the kitchen, or in your bed? Can you turn off your computer or shut down your laptop at the end of your workday?

Second, what are your time boundaries? In my view, it's important that you're not replying late on a Friday night or early on a Sunday morning, as you're setting a dangerous precedent. Do you want to be able to pick up the kids from school at a certain time, or protect your lunch break from being infiltrated by meetings? What's the earliest start time and latest finishing time for you? What is your ideal schedule?

Third, what are your emotional boundaries? Where do you draw the line between what you share online, your personal brand persona, and who you are as an individual in your private life? How involved will you get with your clients? There are lines to be drawn, especially within fields like coaching and therapy, where you can't get too involved.

Fourth, what are your communication boundaries? Do you want people to email you, call you, or WhatsApp you? This then layers onto your time boundaries as to when people can contact you and when they might expect a response. What is the 'escalation protocol' when there is an issue? For example, in a group coaching programme, you might set the expectation that the first port of call is your free Facebook group, then the next regular live Q&A call, and only after that should someone email you directly. Can you have an assistant who takes care of the operational side, including admin and tech support questions, so that you can focus on business-critical tasks?

Finally, what are your own personal boundaries? I'm leaving this one very open, to make space for any other boundaries that are important to you. You have your own personal preferences, purpose, family situation, and health situation. What are your remaining personal boundaries?

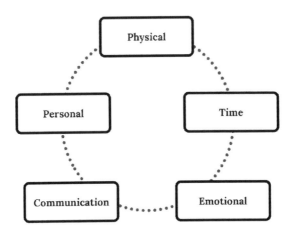

Figure 31: Setting clear boundaries

Communicating your boundaries

Once you've identified your boundaries, using these five different categories, the next step is to communicate them to other people.

It's important to be proactive about this. It's much harder if someone comes to you and complains, "Hey, why haven't you replied to my email?" to suddenly tell them, "Oh, didn't you know, I have this boundary...?" Rather, you must communicate it upfront and be clear on what those non-negotiables are for you.

So, first, you need to think about your audience: who needs to know about your boundaries? Your clients need to know, of course, as well as any freelancers or team members that you're working with; your immediate and maybe also extended family, including your partner and (older) children. Especially when it comes to working from home, where the home and work boundaries are especially blurred, you need to tell the other people living with you what rules apply.

Enforcing your boundaries

Finally, this is not 'one and done'. You'll most likely need to communicate your boundaries again and again, so that you are enforcing your boundaries in a practical sense. It goes without saying that you want to be polite and professional with your clients – and with your family, for that matter – but you do need to be assertive, proactive, and firm.

One example of this is the issue of all the unsolicited "Hey, can I have a quick chat?" or "Can I just pick your brain?" messages that you'll get on LinkedIn as well as from friends and acquaintances. You'll soon realise that a lot of these are either sales pitches or attempts to get your support for free. You'll need to be clear: "Unfortunately, my schedule is quite full – could you tell me more about where you're looking for help?" And then, if it's interesting and relevant, you can send them your booking link. If it's clearly not for you, then a simple, "Unfortunately, my schedule is quite full at the moment, but I look forward to following you here on LinkedIn," for example, should do the trick.

One of the early resources that I produced for my coaching business was on the topic of learning to say "no". It's not just a case of, "Nope!" and that's it; a softer approach can be both appropriate and effective. You can say "no" but offer an alternative. For example, "No, I can't do this Thursday, however, I can do the following Tuesday or Wednesday at these times…" "I can't do that, but I can pass you on to so-and-so who may be able to help." "I can't coach you for free, but here is a list of recommended resources to help you get started." You can also say "yes" but on your own terms. "Yes, I can do that, but not until…" "Yes, I can help you with that, let's discuss in our next scheduled session." "Yes, I'm available, this is my fee…"

Now, I'm not saying that every single one of these boundaries will be set in stone. As of writing, Thursdays are my days for, well, writing this book, and I keep it more-or-less free of calls. However, when my calendar books up and I have a long-standing client who needs a call to make progress on her goals, then I can choose to exceptionally schedule a call on a Thursday. I just need to make sure that the exception doesn't become the rule.

People are more likely to respect your boundaries if they understand that you're able to accommodate them in exceptional circumstances. Just be super clear that you are making an exception and that, next time, it will be on a different day, or there will be an extra charge, or whatever your usual boundary dictates.

However, some of your boundaries will be 'hard nos', meaning that they are non-negotiable. This comes down in large part to your values and what really matters to you.

Remember, embracing the concept of work-life integration does not mean that it all flows into one. You need some structure in place to get the very freedom that you're after. More on this in the next chapter.

Exercise 5-2:

1. Decide on the boundaries you want to set for yourself. Consider:
   a. physical boundaries;
   b. time boundaries;
   c. emotional boundaries;
   d. communication boundaries; and
   e. personal boundaries.

   Determine which boundaries are non-negotiable.
2. Identify who needs to know about these boundaries.
3. What will you need to do to enforce these boundaries?

CREATING SYSTEMS AND PROCESSES

The next step of Pillar 5 is creating systems and processes. I know, it's not sexy, but it is critical in supporting the very freedom that you're after in your life and business. Let me explain...

The freedom that you dream of – this idea of being able to get up and do whatever you want in the morning, and only do work that you love, and be creative and live your best life... – sounds amazing, in theory. The reality, and you may have already experienced this, is that if you allow the pendulum to swing all the way from the rigid corporate structure and micromanaging boss on the one side right over to complete and utter freedom and autonomy on the other... Well, you'll soon find that the days stretch out in front of you. There's no structure to your time, you'll feel lost and unfocused, and you won't get that sense of satisfaction that comes with making progress on your goals.

Yes, spontaneity absolutely has its place, as does rest and going where your energy is. In fact, this complete sense of freedom can be great to experience, for a period, after so many years and even decades without it. However, if you have specific goals, you have your priorities that you've clarified, you have boundaries you want to enforce... then there is a place, an important place, for structure, systems, and processes.

Believe me, I get it – I rebelled against structure and routine in my initial months after quitting my job. However, I soon discovered that processes and systems are, in fact, the things that will free up your time and energy to have that freedom that you want.

If I've managed to convince you, then the question is: what systems do you need to create in order to get the freedom that you want? How can you set up processes, tools, and technology to support you in your endeavours?

Here, I'll share some examples to make this more tangible for you. I can't know exactly what your business looks like, so I'll share examples from my own business and from my experience of working with clients over the past several years, to illustrate the core areas that you probably want to be looking at.

Managing your projects

The first area where you'll need a system is managing the priorities that you've identified for your business.

I've already shared the ideal week tool. Making sure that your priorities are reflected in your calendar, which in turn represents where you're spending your time, is key. A to-do list is all very well, but you want to translate that to-do list into calendar blocks.

When it comes to a to-do list, I would recommend using a digital tool (I use Asana). This makes it much easier to edit, move things around, and not waste time on re-writing or, worse, losing important tasks across different scraps of paper and planners. There are two things that I've done specifically to make this work for me.

The first is that I've grouped all my tasks according to the five project categories that I took you through in a previous chapter: income, visibility, service, operations, and legacy. This really helps me to focus my attention on the right area of my business and make sure that I have a balance across all five areas.

The second is that I've set up recurring tasks. There are tasks that I need to do every day, every week, every month, and setting these up to remind me on that schedule ensures that I maintain my rhythm. I don't have to, every week, every day, sit down and ask, "Okay, what should I be working on today?"

So how are you going to manage your projects? This book, for example, is a particularly complex project with a lot of sub-tasks. Those tasks have included mapping out the structure, coming up with the key points for each section, writing each chapter, editing, and editing again, getting the graphics briefed, proofreading, and proofreading again, and so on.

On- and off-boarding clients

Another area where you'll need a clear process is on- and off-boarding clients. 'On-boarding' in my business means taking a prospective client from first expressing their interest through to getting set up as a client and starting to work with me. The steps here include applying for and scheduling the call; getting a thank you where they can watch a video as to what to expect; receiving the call confirmation; and agreeing to work together and making the payment.

Once they've made that payment, they become a client, and then they'll be taken through a series of steps to get them set up on the membership site and to get our first coaching call scheduled.

So, that's the on-boarding process. The aim is to set your clients up for success, and to reassure them that they have made the right decision in deciding to work with you. The last thing you want is for someone to spend a lot of money with you only to not hear anything, and risk succumbing to 'buyers' remorse'.

The off-boarding happens when they come to the end of their programme. For example, when they finish the Business Academy, they will receive a message congratulating them on completing the initial course with a prompt to upgrade to the next level of coaching. We'll also ask them for feedback and, assuming that feedback is positive, for a testimonial. That's the off-boarding process.

These steps are likely to be manual at first, but, of course, they can also be set up using technology to proceed automatically. And although my own set-up is relatively sophisticated after all these years, the basic steps have been there since the beginning: apply for a call, get it booked in, send the payment link…

Have a think about how you are going to bring people into your business, and how you will say goodbye so that they start and finish with a really exceptional experience.

Managing payment and invoices

A third and very important area is that of payments and accounting. When I first set up my limited company, I did my own accounts using Excel. This was a great way for me to dig in and learn the ins and outs of accounting, but it was very manual and time consuming, and left a lot of room for error. Today, I use a digital tool (FreeAgent); and, of course, I have an accountant.

For ongoing bookkeeping, FreeAgent automatically pulls in my business bank feed, so that I can explain each transaction and label it correctly by category, VAT, and so on. It also generates all the different P&L reports and balance sheets that I need to understand how my business is doing and to complete the annual accounts.

FreeAgent also allows me to create invoices when I receive the Purchase Order from a corporate client. Best of all, it sends automatic email reminders before each invoice is due and once it becomes overdue. Late payments are a huge issue for freelancers and business owners in the UK, and this at least helps you keep on top of the worst culprits.

Individual clients will buy my programmes directly on the website with either an upfront or a monthly option. This is done via a payment software called Stripe and then invoices are generated automatically as well.

It's a fundamental premise of a business that you need to have a means by which people can pay you, and you'll want to stay on top of your bookkeeping and accounts to ensure that you're compliant and that you're not hit with an unexpected tax bill at the end of the year.

Creating and repurposing content

We talked a lot about content in Pillar 4, when we looked at personal branding, and there are a few different elements to consider here when it comes to processes.

Remember the 3Ps? Plan – Produce – Promote. You'll have your content themes and weekly topics planned out, as well as what formats you need to create on a regular basis. This might be videos or podcast episodes, written articles and posts, emails, and so on. Then you'll want to block time to batch create that planned content and repurpose it into different formats. In my case, this includes sending the podcast recording off to my audio editor as well as getting it transcribed (which I currently do via AI software, Otter.ai). We use Canva Pro, in which we've created a brand kit with all my logos, colours, fonts, and images, and we can then create visual content that's fully on brand using a set of pre-designed templates. Finally, you'll need to have a way to systematically schedule and share the content on your channels.

Each of these steps is now set up as a recurring task in Asana, my project management software. Although it seems like a huge amount of content, and I do keep evolving what we do and how we do it, it has by now become second nature for me to plan, produce, and promote the content and it's a pretty well-oiled machine.

Welcoming new email subscribers

Finally, we talked about welcoming clients; what about welcoming new email subscribers?

A classic marketing mechanism that entrepreneurs use is to create a resource – this might be a PDF, or video, or a little email series – that you offer to prospects for free in return for their email address. Then that person will receive the download along with a sequence of emails that provides a bit more information and support and moves them along to the next step, which is to work with you in some form or another.

In my case, you might have seen my free business assessment, which is a scorecard based on the 5 Pillars that I'm taking you through in this book. You can download this resource at onestepoutside.com/scorecard. When you sign up, you will receive an initial email, "Hello, here's the resource that you requested, and here's a little more about who I am…" Then there is a sequence of emails sharing what I hope is useful content, followed by details about my paid programmes, and an invitation to book a call with me.

At the time of writing, having your own email list and community that you effectively 'own' – versus the 'rented' land you might have on social media platforms – is still a crucial part of your ecosystem. Having an email series like this is an important way of welcoming new subscribers, letting them find out more about who you are and what you do, and giving them clear next steps to follow if they're looking for more help.

I have given examples here of tools that I'm currently using, although I'm reluctant to do so as these can quickly become out of date. For an up-to-date overview of the tools that I'm using, visit the resources page on my website onestepoutside.com.

However, it's important not to get caught up in the tech. Always start by having a think about what you need; then you can look at which tool is right for you. You can always start manually at first – but do make sure that you document your processes, so that you can easily automate or outsource later.

Exercise 5-3:

1. List the processes that you want to start documenting.
2. How will you keep track of your important projects and tasks?
3. What templates do you need to create?
4. What tools will you need to invest in to simplify things?

DELEGATING AND OUTSOURCING

We're onto the final step of the final pillar. I've hinted at this one already: we're talking about delegating and outsourcing.

As ever, I stand on the shoulders of giants with another powerful quote for you from someone far more successful than me, this time, Richard Branson (2017):

> *If you really want to grow as an entrepreneur, you've got to learn to delegate.*

Whether you think of yourself as an eternal freelancer or solopreneur, or you have a vision of growing a larger team, I completely subscribe to this view: you must learn to delegate. There are reasons why you might find this difficult, however.

A first hesitation is, "I can't afford to pay for help (yet)." It can feel uncomfortable to invest in support, especially when you aren't earning a lot of money in your business, and you might feel like you should be doing everything yourself.

A second hesitation is, perhaps more subconsciously, "No one else can do it as well as I can." When it's your own business, and especially if you're a perfectionist, it can be hard to let go of control. Let's face it, there will always be teething problems at the start, and it might take you a few different attempts to find someone who is a good fit.

Third, "I don't even know how to go about finding, and hiring, someone." Do you go via an agency or advertise yourself? Do you go global or local? Whichever route you choose, it does take time and energy to find the right person to support you.

I'm sure there are other reasons why you might hold back from delegating and outsourcing tasks in your business; but you will need to challenge these beliefs and get comfortable with delegating early on in your business. You want to be doing the work that you love – this is the reason why you started the business in the first place. You want to be focusing on your 'zone of genius', the things that you're good at. And you need to be focusing on things like business development and strategy and doing the work that your clients are paying you for, not wasting your time on back-end admin work that doesn't add a whole lot of value.

This is the way you must think about it: what work are you currently doing that someone else could do faster, better, or cheaper? If you could learn how to do something but it would take you a long time first to learn and then to muddle through it, then it's worth paying someone else to do it more quickly. If someone is better at something than you, if they're an expert and you're not, then that's an obvious case of outsourcing to somebody who will do a better job. Finally, if you can charge £100 for an hour of client work, then it's a no brainer to pay someone else £20 to free up that time for you to focus on your client work.

Before you outsource

A brief warning here before we get into more concrete examples of things you could be outsourcing. Make sure you know what you're doing, and you've done the due diligence of documenting your processes and systems upfront – see the previous chapter – before you try to hire someone else to do it for you. If you don't know what it is you're asking someone to do, things will quickly get very messy, or expensive.

I recommend recording your screen as you go about doing your regular tasks in your business. For example, I would record and narrate as I formatted and scheduled a blog post and then I'd share that recording with my freelancer so that she could follow the steps. As you do this for the different areas of your business, you'll end up with a set of Standard Operating Procedures, or SOPs.

Unfortunately, things do keep changing, so these SOPs will need updating. This is, of course, something that your team member can do as and when needed. When this person leaves your business, you can also ask them to onboard their replacement.

What you should outsource first

Let's look at a few examples, and a few different types of tasks that you might considering outsourcing. We'll look at three different categories:

- simple and repetitive tasks;
- tasks that require expertise; and
- personal tasks.

Simple and repetitive tasks

The first area where I'd encourage you to start is offloading the most simple, repetitive, and mundane tasks. For example, when I started outsourcing work to a freelancer, I had her formatting and scheduling blog articles, social media content, and regular email newsletters. You might also consider briefing them on a simple piece of research, such as a competitive analysis, where you give them a list of businesses or entrepreneurs and they can provide you with an overview of different aspects that you're interested in. You might ask them to come up with a list of podcasts along with contact information for pitching yourself as a possible guest. You can also have them be responsible for tracking results, whether that be weekly or monthly metrics.

My own first experience of outsourcing was a revelation. When I first hired someone to take care of the blog post and social media scheduling, even just for a few hours a week, I suddenly had a whole lot of free time. This was quite a wake-up call for me. I realised that I had been spending my week doing 'busy work', a lot of back-end, operational tasks, rather than focusing on the strategic priorities that would truly move the needle in my business.

Remember the priorities from the start of Pillar 5: yes, there is operational work to be done, but I also need to be doing income-generating activities and I need to be working on my visibility, not just sitting there behind my computer scheduling blog posts and social media content. As soon as I offloaded those simple, repetitive tasks, I freed up time in my calendar to create content – including, recently, developing my Business Academy course, and writing this book – because I have someone else who's doing the day-to-day work for me.

So, this first category is simple, repetitive tasks that anyone can do; and I really mean *anyone*. You don't need to, and probably shouldn't, hire someone with a lot of experience at this stage. You're looking for somebody at a basic 'virtual assistant' kind of level, perhaps someone straight out of university; someone who you can teach. You're going to give them those videos that you've recorded and they're going to follow along, step by step. This becomes the category of tasks that a more junior person can do more cheaply than you can.

Tasks that require expertise

The second category includes the tasks that someone else can do better than you.

An obvious area here is accounting. Professional accountants will help you avoid paying unnecessary tax or missing important deadlines, while drawing the most tax-efficient salary. Working with a chartered accountant on top of your accounting software (like FreeAgent) is a great solution for your finances.

Another area might be graphic design. Personally, I am not a designer. Yes, I can do some simple social media templates and headers using a tool like Canva, but I wouldn't dream of trying to create a logo. If I want a professional-looking resource, I will have someone else create it for me.

Along the same lines, another area is web design and development. Now, I did create and manage my own WordPress website for many years, using a combination of ready-made themes and templates, a little tech savvy, and a willingness to learn a bit of html and CSS. If you lack the time or inclination to learn, however, then investing in an agency or freelancer here is money well spent.

Next, copywriting. I am a writer, albeit not a copywriter specifically, so I do choose to do all my writing myself;

however, if this is not your strong suit, then this can be a really important area to outsource.

Editing the audio of my podcasts is highly technical work that I tried and failed to learn and quickly handed off to someone far more talented than me.

Video editing. I keep editing to a minimum with free software that comes with my Mac, but, again, if you're after a more professional look, then you might consider an expert here.

Search engine optimisation, SEO, is another important area. There are WordPress plug-ins that can help here, for example, I use the Yoast premium plug-in to optimise my posts. I did already have a basic understanding of SEO from my corporate marketing days; you might prefer to work with an agency to optimise your content from day one.

Personal tasks

The final category, not to be neglected, is your personal life. Professional childcare is one way of delegating. At the time of writing, my two kids are at nursery three days a week; without that support, I wouldn't be able to have a functioning business. Likewise, paying a cleaner, let's say, £12 an hour, is worth it if you can earn £100 (or more) in that hour in your business; not to mention the arguments you will avoid with your spouse. Ironing, dry cleaning, maybe even general housekeeping – these things can all be outsourced to free up your time and energy to focus on what really matters to you.

Now, yes, you may not be able to afford all this support from day one in your business and, in fact, I would caution against throwing too much money at professional help before you even have a proven business model and a pipeline of clients. You can have a functioning business with a very basic set-up when you're first starting out, and the 'fun' things like fancy websites, business cards, and automations aren't going to make a difference at this stage. What I am saying, however, is that you should start tentatively outsourcing early on in your business so that you get used to it, and then layer on additional support as you go, and as you grow.

I know it can be uncomfortable, especially when you're first starting out and you feel you can't afford to invest, or you're not ready to let go. It's simply not possible to grow a business – take it from me, and my own painful experience – if you're spending all your time doing these little things that someone else could, and should, be doing instead.

So, get started, and get into the habit of delegating, however tentatively; and remember the previous step of first documenting your systems and processes. Even if you're not yet ready to hire someone, at least get things set up in the meantime, so that you're prepared to press that button when you are ready.

Ultimately, you're trying to build a business here that you love – a life that you love – and so you get to decide where and how you spend your time. Yes, there will always be some things that you do need to do, even if you don't want to. There are also going to be a lot of things that you don't have to do, and that you absolutely can hand off to someone else.

You don't have to – and I certainly don't want to – have a physical office with a team of people on the payroll. Instead, think about building your dream team with a flexible network of freelancers and experts to support you in creating the life and business that you want.

With this final look at delegating and outsourcing, we've finished Pillar 5, designing flexible work-life integration; and we've finished all of the 5 Pillars.

Exercise 5-4:

1. Identify the things that someone else can do faster, better, or cheaper than you can. Consider:
    a. things you want to do (and don't want to delegate);
    b. things you have to do (and can't delegate); and
    c. things someone else could or should do.

2. For the things that someone else could or should be doing, whom do you need to delegate this to? And is it a one-off project or ongoing?

Moving forwards

MOVING FORWARDS

If you're anything like me, you will have eagerly devoured the book, but you will have done so quite passively. (No? Have you completed all the exercises? Are the margins full of notes? Do you have a clear plan for your business now?) Personally, I can count on one hand the number of books that I've annotated, and where I've taken action on the prompts from the author.

A book – and this book, I hope – is an incredible resource. But it is just information. And, if you leave it there on the page, it will do absolutely nothing for you in terms of business results or life satisfaction.

So, what can you do? Well, first, if you have just been flicking through the book, or even if you've read it quite thoroughly, I'd encourage you to go back through the book. Read it again. Highlight key sections. Take notes. Fold down the corners. The book really is intended to be a practical guide, and I'd encourage you to use it as such.

If you want to work through the material in the book in a more interactive way, then I'd invite you to buy my course, the Outsiders Business Academy. If you've read the book, you'll know all about this, as I've talked about it quite a bit. It's a self-paced course that walks you through the 5 Pillars with a set of videos and worksheets. You can register and start learning at onestepoutside.com/course.

Whether you take the course or stick with the book, there is one thing I need you to do. Take action. Implement what you're learning. Choose an ideal client, update your LinkedIn headline and bio, and go out there and talk to people. The biggest mistake you can make is to keep putting it off, keep procrastinating, tweaking your elevator pitch, or playing around with your packages. Do something, put it out there, and then adapt as you learn what's working and what needs tweaking. Know that there is no right answer – and, if there is, it's up to you to find it.

Here's to building a life and business outside of the 9 to 5 – and achieving success on your terms.

Further resources

GETTING MORE SUPPORT

Listen to the Reimagining Success podcast

Every week, you'll be getting a mix of inspirational, thought-provoking episodes, and more practical, actionable strategies and tips to help you build a life outside of the 9 to 5.

Listen now:
reimaginingsuccesspodcast.com

Get a free assessment of your business

Download this scorecard to review where you are on each of the 5 Pillars of building a life outside of the 9 to 5 and get clear action steps to help you fill the gaps.

Download the free scorecard:
onestepoutside.com/scorecard

Work through the materials in a structured course

The Outsiders Business Academy is a self-paced course for you to work through in your own time, to learn – and implement – the foundations of building a profitable business that lets you escape the 9 to 5.

Register and start learning now:
onestepoutside.com/course

Join our accelerator mastermind

Once you've worked through either the book or the course, you'll be eligible to apply for the Outsiders Business Accelerator. This is a group programme that will allow you to continue implementing what you've learned and move on to more advanced strategies.

Join us:
onestepoutside.com/accelerate

Individual coaching and mentoring

If you're looking for one-to-one support to help you achieve your specific life and business goals, I have a limited number of spots for individual coaching and mentoring.

Book a call to discuss your goals: onestepoutside.com/call

RECOMMENDED READING

My favourite books…

…on redefining success

Beck, M. (2003) *Finding Your Own North Star: How to Claim the Life You were Meant to Live*. London: Piatkus.

Ferris, T. (2011) *The 4-Hour Work Week: Escape the 9-5, Live Anywhere and Join the New Rich*. London: Vermilon.

García, H. and Miralles, F. (2017) *Ikigai: The Japanese Secret to a Long and Happy Life*. London: Hutchinson.

Guillebeau, C. (2010) *The Art of Non-Conformity: Set Your Own Rules, Live the Life You Want, and Change the World*. [s.l.]: TarcherPerigee.

Laporte, D. (2014) *The Desire Map: A Guide to Creating Goals with Soul*. [s.l.]: Sounds True.

…on confidence and resilience

Acuff, J. (2021) *Soundtracks: The Surprising Solution to Overthinking*. Grand Rapids, Michigan: Baker Books.

Clark, D. (2021) *The Long Game: How to be a Long-term Thinker in a Short-term World*. Boston, Massachusetts: Harvard Business Review Press.

Dweck, C. (2017) *Mindset: Changing the Way You Think to Fulfil Your Potential*. New York: Ballantine Books.

Godin, S. (2012) *The Icarus Deception: How high will you fly?* London: Portfolio Penguin.

Pressfield, S. (2012) *The War of Art: Break Through the Blocks and Win Your Inner Creative Battles*. New York: Black Irish Entertainment LLC.

…on business models

Church, P., Cook, P. and Stein, S. (2016) *The Thought Leaders Practice*. Balgowlah, NSW: Thought Leaders Publishing.

Duffield-Thomas, D. (2020) *Chillpreneur: The New Rules for Creating Success, Freedom, and Abundance on Your Terms*. London: Hay House UK Ltd.

Hopson, B. and Ledger, K. (2009) *And What Do You Do?: 10 Steps to Creating a Portfolio Career*. London: A&C Black Publishers.

Michalowicz, M. (2017) *Profit First: Transform Your Business from a Cash-Eating Monster to a Money-Making Machine*. New York: Portfolio Penguin.

Williams, J. (2010) *Screw Work, Let's Play: Do What You Love and Get Paid for It*. Harlow: Pearson Education Ltd.

…on personal branding

Clark, D. (2017) *Reinventing You: Define Your Brand, Imagine Your Future*. Boston, Massachusetts: Harvard Business Review Press.

Ducker, C. (2018) *Rise of the Youpreneur: The Definitive Guide to Becoming the Go-To Leader in Your Industry and Building a Future-Proof Business*. Cambridge: 4C Press.

Huntbach, M., Cambridge, L. and Sheridan, M. (2020) *Content Fortress: A Simple Content Marketing Strategy that Helps You Attract Customers You'll LOVE to do Business with*. [s.l.]: Independently published.

Priestley, D. (2014) *Key Person of Influence: The Five-Step Method to Become One of the Most Highly Valued and Highly Paid People in Your Industry*. [s.l.]: Rethink Press.

Schaefer, M. (2017) *KNOWN: The handbook for building and unleashing your personal brand in the digital age*. [s.l.]: Schaefer Marketing Solutions.

...on work-life integration

Burkeman, O. (2022) *Four Thousand Weeks: Time Managements for Mortals.* London: Vintage.

Clear, J. (2018) *Atomic Habits: Tiny Changes, Remarkable Results.* London: Random House Business.

McKeown, G. (2014) *Essentialism: The Disciplined Pursuit of Less.* London: Virgin Books.

Newport, C. (2016) *Deep Work: Rules for Focused Success in a Distracted World.* London: Piatkus.

Rodsky, E. (2022) *Find Your Unicorn Space: Reclaim Your Creative Life in a Too-Busy World.* [s.l.]: Hachette Australia.

References

REFERENCES

Basu, A. (2016) *Today in the Quote*. Available at: https://twitter.com/arbastrategies/status/755811068123938820?cxt=HHwWiICwja-Kl_0UAAAA (Accessed: 22 October 2022).

Branson, R. (2017) *Richard Branson on Learning to Delegate*. Available at: https://teamreferralnetwork.com/news/2015/02/richard-branson-on-learning-to-delegate/ (Accessed: 22 October 2022).

Covey, S. (2020) *The 7 Habits of Highly Effective People* 30th Anniversary Edition. New York: Simon & Schuster UK.

Csikszentmihalyi, M. (2002) *Flow: The Psychology of Happiness* London: Rider.

Dweck, C. (2017) *Mindset: Changing the way you think to fulfil your potential*. New York: Robinson.

Dyson, B. (1991) *Coca-Cola's Secret Formula for Success: Vision, Confidence and Luck*. Available at: https://www.markturner.net/wp-content/uploads/2015/05/Whistle-Brian_Dyson-Georgia_Tech_Commencement_Sept_1991-p3.pdf (Accessed: 22 October 2022).

Expert Program Management (2018) *Business Model Canvas Explained*. Available at: https://expertprogrammanagement.com/2018/10/business-model-canvas-explained/ (Accessed: 11 November 2022).

Frankl, V. (2004) *Man's Search for Meaning*. London: Rider.

García, H. and Miralles, F. (2017) *Ikigai: The Japanese Secret to a Long and Happy Life*. London: Hutchinson.

Gerber, M. (2001) *The E-Myth Revisited*. New York: HarperBus.

Godin, S. (2009) *define: Brand.* Available at: https://seths.blog/2009/12/define-brand/ (Accessed: 22 October 2022).

Godin, S. (2013) *Three questions to ask your marketing team.* Available at: https://seths.blog/2013/09/three-questions-to-ask-your-marketing-team/ (Accessed: 10 November 2022).

Huffington, A. (2020) *Why This is the Perfect Time to Redefine Success.* Available at: https://thriveglobal.com/stories/arianna-huffington-now-perfect-time-redefine-success-meaningful-work/ (Accessed: 22 October 2022).

Keller, H. (2010) *Optimism: An Essay.* Available at: https://www.gutenberg.org/files/31622/31622-h/31622-h.htm (Accessed: 11 November 2022).

Kukral, J. (2006) *Your brand is not what Google says it is.* Available at: https://www.marketingprofs.com/opinions/2006/15033/your-brand-is-not-what-google-says-it-is (Accessed: 11 November 2022).

Lafley, A. G. and Charan, R. (2008) *The consumer is boss.* Available at: https://archive.fortune.com/2008/03/07/news/companies/lafley_charan.fortune/index.htm (Accessed: 11 November 2022).

Laporte, D. (2014) *The Desire Map: A Guide to Creating Goals with Soul.* [s.l.]: Sounds True.

Lundberg, A. (2018) *Leaving the Corporate 9 to 5: Stories from people who've done it (and how you can too!).* London: One Step Outside.

Obama, B. (2009) *Text of President Obama's School Speech.* Available at: https://abcnews.go.com/Politics/president-obamas-back-school-message-students/story?id=8509426 (Accessed: 11 November 2022).

Rodsky, E. (2022) *Find Your Unicorn Space: Reclaim Your Creative Life in a Too-Busy World* [s.l.]: Hachette Australia.

Tracy, B. (2013) *Eat that Frog!* London: Hodder Paperbacks.

Winn, M. (2014) *What is your ikigai?* Available at: https://theviewinside.me/what-is-your-ikigai/ (Accessed: 11 November 2022).

Zuzunaga, A. (2011) *Propósito*. Available at: https://www.cosmograma.com/proposito.php (Accessed: 11 November 2022).

About the Author

ABOUT THE AUTHOR

Anna Lundberg is the founder of One Step Outside™, where she helps experienced professionals around the world design a career, a business and a lifestyle that brings them more freedom, flexibility, and fulfilment – outside of the conventional 9 to 5.

Voted 'most likely to succeed' and graduating top of her class aged 17, Anna studied Philosophy, Politics and Economics (PPE) at the University of Oxford and then continued on to do a post-graduate degree in International Relations at the Graduate Institute of International Studies in Geneva.

Having 'ended up' in corporate marketing after her studies, she spent the formative years of her career in beauty and luxury brand management. Leaving her role at multinational Procter & Gamble to start her own company in 2013, she began her new entrepreneurial path by providing digital marketing consulting to well-known luxury brands through to exciting new start-ups and solopreneurs.

Anna now combines more than a decade of experience in corporate marketing with her training in coaching and positive psychology techniques to help people reimagine the next phase of their career, with a blend of life coaching and business mentoring.

She is the host of the Reimagining Success™ podcast and author of *Leaving the Corporate 9 to 5*.

Printed in Great Britain
by Amazon